At Sylvan, we believe that everyone can master math skills, and we are glad you have chosen our resources to help your children experience the joy of mathematics as they build crucial reasoning skills. We know that time spent reinforcing lessons learned in school will contribute to understanding and mastery.

Success in math requires more than just memorizing basic facts and algorithms; it also requires children to make connections between the real world and math concepts in order to solve problems. Successful problem solvers will be ready for the challenges of mathematics as they advance to more complex topics and encounter new problems both in school and at home.

We use a research-based, step-by-step process in teaching math at Sylvan that includes thought-provoking math problems and activities. As students increase their success as problem solvers, they become more confident. With increasing confidence, students build even more success. The design of the Sylvan workbooks lays out a roadmap for mathematical learning that is designed to lead your child to success in school.

We're excited to partner with you to support the development of a confident, well-prepared independent learner!

The Sylvan Team

Sylvan Learning Center
Unleash your child's potential here

No matter how big or small the academic challenge, every child has the ability to learn. But sometimes children need help making it happen. Sylvan believes every child has the potential to do great things. And we know better than anyone else how to tap into that academic potential so that a child's future really is full of possibilities. Sylvan Learning Center is the place where your child can build and master the learning skills needed to succeed and unlock the potential you know is there.

The proven, personalized approach of our in-center programs deliver unparalleled results that other supplemental education services simply can't match. Your child's achievements will be seen not only in test scores and report cards but outside the classroom as well. And when he starts achieving his full potential, everyone will know it. You will see a new level of confidence come through in everything he does and every interaction he has.

How can Sylvan's personalized in-center approach help your child unleash his potential?

• Starting with our exclusive Sylvan Skills Assessment®, we pinpoint your child's exact academic needs.

• Then we develop a customized learning plan designed to achieve your child's academic goals.

• Through our method of skill mastery, your child will not only learn and master every skill in his personalized plan, he will be truly motivated and inspired to achieve his full potential.

To get started, simply contact your local Sylvan Learning Center to set up an appointment. And to learn more about Sylvan and our innovative in-center programs, call 1-800-EDUCATE or visit www.SylvanLearning.com. *With over 750 locations in North America, there is a Sylvan Learning Center near you!*

5th Grade
Basic Math Success
Workbook

Published in the United States by Random House, Inc., New York, and in Canada by Random House of Canada Limited, Toronto.

This book was previously published with the title *5th Grade Basic Math Success* as a trade paperback by Sylvan Learning, Inc., an imprint of Penguin Random House LLC, in 2010.

www.sylvanlearning.com

Created by Smarterville Productions LLC
Producer & Editorial Direction: The Linguistic Edge
Producer: TJ Trochlil McGreevy
Writer: Amy Kraft
Cover and Interior Illustrations: Shawn Finley and Duendes del Sur
Cover Design: Suzanne Lee
Layout and Art Direction: SunDried Penguin
Director of Product Development: Russell Ginns

First Edition

ISBN: 978-0-375-43045-9

Library of Congress Cataloging-in-Publication Data available upon request.

This book is available at special discounts for bulk purchases for sales promotions or premiums.
For more information, write to Special Markets/Premium Sales, 1745 Broadway, MD 6-2,
New York, New York 10019 or e-mail specialmarkets@randomhouse.com.

PRINTED IN CHINA

10 9 8 7 6

Contents

Contents

Measurement & Geometry

Pattern Patch

MULTIPLY each number by the first number, and WRITE the missing numbers in each pattern.

Example:

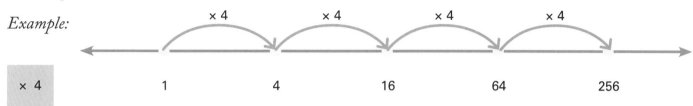

× 4

1   4   16   64   256

1.

× 2

2   4

2.

× 2

3   48

3.

× 3

1   3

4.

× 3

2   162

5.

× 5

1   625

Multiplication Patterns

So Many Zeros

Factors are numbers that are being multiplied together, and the **product** is the result.

Find the product of the first number in each factor. Next, count the total number of zeros in both factors. Write the same number of zeros after the product of the first numbers.

30	×	500	=	_____
3	×	5	=	15
30	×	500	=	_____
30	×	500	=	15,000

3	×	5	=	15
3	×	50	=	150
30	×	50	=	1,500
30	×	500	=	15,000
300	×	500	=	150,000
300	×	5,000	=	1,500,000

WRITE the products.

1.
8	×	1	=	_____
8	×	10	=	_____
80	×	10	=	_____
80	×	100	=	_____
800	×	100	=	_____
800	×	1,000	=	_____

2.
6	×	7	=	_____
6	×	70	=	_____
60	×	70	=	_____
60	×	700	=	_____
600	×	700	=	_____
600	×	7,000	=	_____

3.
2	×	3	=	_____
2	×	30	=	_____
20	×	30	=	_____
20	×	300	=	_____
200	×	300	=	_____
200	×	3,000	=	_____

4.
4	×	9	=	_____
4	×	90	=	_____
40	×	90	=	_____
40	×	900	=	_____
400	×	900	=	_____
400	×	9,000	=	_____

Picture It

Use the pictures to help you answer the problems. WRITE each product.

Example: 43 × 6 = ____240____

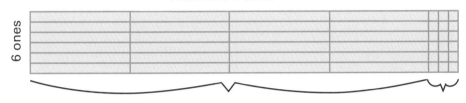

4 tens and 3 ones

6 ones

4 tens × 6 ones = 24 tens, or 240   3 ones × 6 ones = 18 ones, or 18

When multiplying a two-digit number, think of it as tens and ones.
240 + 18 = 258
43 × 6 = 258

1. 56 × 3 = _____

2. 65 × 7 = _____

3. 49 × 8 = _____

Computation Station

Multiply a three-digit number by a one-digit number.

| 2 283 × 8 4 Multiply the ones. 3 × 8 = 24 | 6 2 283 × 8 64 Multiply the tens. 80 × 8 = 640 640 + 20 = 660 | 6 283 × 8 2,264 Multiply the hundreds. 200 × 8 = 1,600 1,600 + 600 = 2,200 |

WRITE each product.

1. 45
    × 3

2. 52
    × 6

3. 13
    × 7

4. 74
    × 4

5. 68
    × 8

6. 34
    × 5

7. 227
    × 7

8. 589
    × 2

9. 644
    × 5

10. 356
    × 8

11. 995
    × 7

12. 447
    × 4

13. 739
    × 9

14. 253
    × 6

15. 172
    × 8

16. 929
    × 4

17. 684
    × 5

18. 865
    × 9

Computation Station

Multiply a two-digit number by a two-digit number.

$\overset{4}{9}7$ $\times\ \ 46$ $\overline{582}$	$\overset{2}{9}7$ $\times\ \ 46$ $\overline{582}$ $\ \ 80$	$\overset{2}{9}7$ $\times\ \ 46$ $\overline{582}$ $3,880$	97 $\times\ \ 46$ $\overline{582}$ $+\ 3,880$ $\overline{4,462}$
Multiply 97 by 6.	Multiply 97 by 40, starting with the ones place. $7 \times 40 = 280$	Next, multiply the tens place. $90 \times 40 = 3,600$ $3,600 + 200 = 3,800$	Then add 582 and 3,880.

WRITE each product.

1. $\begin{array}{r} 27 \\ \times\ 20 \\ \hline \end{array}$
2. $\begin{array}{r} 66 \\ \times\ 32 \\ \hline \end{array}$
3. $\begin{array}{r} 45 \\ \times\ 14 \\ \hline \end{array}$
4. $\begin{array}{r} 56 \\ \times\ 28 \\ \hline \end{array}$
5. $\begin{array}{r} 92 \\ \times\ 19 \\ \hline \end{array}$
6. $\begin{array}{r} 31 \\ \times\ 36 \\ \hline \end{array}$

7. $\begin{array}{r} 72 \\ \times\ 47 \\ \hline \end{array}$
8. $\begin{array}{r} 87 \\ \times\ 53 \\ \hline \end{array}$
9. $\begin{array}{r} 50 \\ \times\ 26 \\ \hline \end{array}$
10. $\begin{array}{r} 44 \\ \times\ 39 \\ \hline \end{array}$
11. $\begin{array}{r} 68 \\ \times\ 58 \\ \hline \end{array}$
12. $\begin{array}{r} 18 \\ \times\ 17 \\ \hline \end{array}$

13. $\begin{array}{r} 94 \\ \times\ 52 \\ \hline \end{array}$
14. $\begin{array}{r} 81 \\ \times\ 34 \\ \hline \end{array}$
15. $\begin{array}{r} 75 \\ \times\ 15 \\ \hline \end{array}$
16. $\begin{array}{r} 67 \\ \times\ 65 \\ \hline \end{array}$
17. $\begin{array}{r} 99 \\ \times\ 59 \\ \hline \end{array}$
18. $\begin{array}{r} 84 \\ \times\ 78 \\ \hline \end{array}$

Computation Station

Multiply a three-digit number by a two-digit number.

$$\begin{array}{r}{\scriptstyle 3\ 1}\\ 963\\ \times\ \ 5\ 6\\ \hline 5{,}7\ 7\ 8\end{array}$$	$$\begin{array}{r}{\scriptstyle 1}\\ 963\\ \times\ \ 5\ 6\\ \hline 5{,}7\ 7\ 8\\ 5\ 0\end{array}$$	$$\begin{array}{r}{\scriptstyle 3\ 1}\\ 963\\ \times\ \ 5\ 6\\ \hline 5{,}7\ 7\ 8\\ 1\ 5\ 0\end{array}$$	$$\begin{array}{r}{\scriptstyle 3\ 1}\\ 963\\ \times\ \ 5\ 6\\ \hline 5{,}7\ 7\ 8\\ 48{,}1\ 5\ 0\end{array}$$	$$\begin{array}{r}{\scriptstyle 3\ 1}\\ 963\\ \times\ \ 5\ 6\\ \hline 5{,}7\ 7\ 8\\ +48{,}1\ 5\ 0\\ \hline 5\ 3{,}9\ 2\ 8\end{array}$$
Multiply 963 by 6.	Multiply 963 by 50, starting with the ones place. $3 \times 50 = 150$	Next, multiply the tens place. $60 \times 50 = 3{,}000$ $3{,}000 + 100 = 3{,}100$	Next, multiply the hundreds place. $900 \times 50 = 45{,}000$ $45{,}000 + 3{,}000 = 48{,}000$	Then add 5,778 and 48,150.

WRITE each product.

1. $$\begin{array}{r}325\\ \times\ 61\end{array}$$

2. $$\begin{array}{r}478\\ \times\ 93\end{array}$$

3. $$\begin{array}{r}932\\ \times\ 58\end{array}$$

4. $$\begin{array}{r}215\\ \times\ 87\end{array}$$

5. $$\begin{array}{r}559\\ \times\ 74\end{array}$$

6. $$\begin{array}{r}737\\ \times\ 67\end{array}$$

7. $$\begin{array}{r}530\\ \times\ 49\end{array}$$

8. $$\begin{array}{r}197\\ \times\ 34\end{array}$$

9. $$\begin{array}{r}812\\ \times\ 91\end{array}$$

10. $$\begin{array}{r}385\\ \times\ 29\end{array}$$

11. $$\begin{array}{r}497\\ \times\ 55\end{array}$$

12. $$\begin{array}{r}664\\ \times\ 83\end{array}$$

13. $$\begin{array}{r}344\\ \times\ 96\end{array}$$

14. $$\begin{array}{r}939\\ \times\ 78\end{array}$$

15. $$\begin{array}{r}502\\ \times\ 27\end{array}$$

16. $$\begin{array}{r}463\\ \times\ 54\end{array}$$

17. $$\begin{array}{r}689\\ \times\ 33\end{array}$$

18. $$\begin{array}{r}925\\ \times\ 62\end{array}$$

Computation Station

Multiply a four-digit number by a three-digit number.

^{1 2 2} 4,3 7 8 × 2 5 3 ——— 1 3,1 3 4	^{1 3 4} 4,3 7 8 × 2 5 3 ——— 1 3,1 3 4 2 1 8,9 0 0	^{1 1} 4,3 7 8 × 2 5 3 ——— 1 3,1 3 4 2 1 8,9 0 0 8 7 5,6 0 0	4,3 7 8 × 2 5 3 ——— 1 3,1 3 4 2 1 8,9 0 0 +8 7 5,6 0 0 ——— 1,1 0 7,6 3 4
Multiply 4,378 by 3.	Multiply 4,378 by 50.	Multiply 4,378 by 200.	Then add 13,134 + 218,900 + 875,600.

WRITE each product.

1. 1,546
   × 84

2. 6,115
   × 27

3. 4,923
   × 66

4. 8,354
   × 52

5. 3,694
   × 93

6.   677
   × 352

7.   962
   × 175

8.   407
   × 486

9.   726
   × 296

10.   595
   × 510

11. 5,204
   × 268

12. 7,328
   × 350

13. 3,831
   × 193

14. 2,456
   × 679

15. 9,197
   × 437

Many Miles

WRITE the answers.

HINT: Multiply the number of miles by the number of days in the month.

If Marissa rides the same number of miles each day for a month or a year, how many miles would she ride?

1. 8 miles × 31 days = ___248___ miles

2. 11 miles × 28 days = _____ miles

3. 26 miles × 31 days = _____ miles

4. 32 miles × 30 days = _____ miles

5. 40 miles × 31 days = _____ miles

6. 45 miles × 30 days = _____ miles

7. 4 miles × 365 days = _____ miles

8. 15 miles × 365 days = _____ miles

9. 24 miles × 365 days = _____ miles

10. 29 miles × 365 days = _____ miles

11. 37 miles × 365 days = _____ miles

12. 50 miles × 365 days = _____ miles

Round About

Rounding numbers can help you estimate a product.

6,893	→	7,000	6,893 rounded to the nearest thousand is 7,000.
× 795	→	× 800	795 rounded to the nearest hundred is 800.
		5,600,000	7,000 × 800 = 5,600,000
			6,893 × 795 = 5,479,935

ESTIMATE each product by rounding to the first digit and multiplying. WRITE the actual product to check your estimate.

1. 296
    × 24   × _____

2. 814
    × 96   × _____

3. 571
    × 935   × _____

4. 707
    × 682   × _____

5. 4,338
    × 472   × _____

6. 9,566
    × 343   × _____

The Mighty Marlock

The Mighty Marlock will guess any product, but he sometimes guesses incorrectly. ESTIMATE each product, and CROSS OUT any product that is clearly wrong.

$775 \times 91 = 70,525$

$6,323 \times 972 = 6,145,956$

$199 \times 485 = 96,515$

$611 \times 281 = 1,821,851$

$2,594 \times 312 = 2,637,208$

$836 \times 17 = 44,952$

Tic-Tac-Toe

CIRCLE any number that is a factor of the blue number. PUT an X through any number that is not a factor. DRAW a line when you find three factors in a row. The line can go across, down, or diagonally.

Example:

50

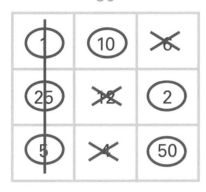

1	×	50	=	50
25	×	2	=	50
5	×	10	=	50

The factors of 50 are 1, 2, 5, 10, 25, and 50.

12

3	7	5
8	6	4
12	10	2

18

4	1	2
12	8	9
3	10	6

24

14	12	16
9	5	4
6	8	3

40

4	6	5
12	20	10
2	3	7

Factors

So Much in Common

A factor shared by two or more numbers is called a **common factor**. The **greatest common factor** is the largest number in a set of common factors.

Example: The factors of 12 are 1, 2, 3, 4, 6, and 12.
The factors of 30 are 1, 2, 3, 5, 6, 10, 15, and 30.

The common factors of 12 and 30 are 1, 2, 3, and 6.
The greatest common factor is 6.

WRITE the factors of each pair of numbers followed by the common factors and the greatest common factor.

14: ☐, ☐, ☐, ☐

49: ☐, ☐, ☐

Common factors: ☐, ☐

Greatest common factor: ☐

20: ☐, ☐, ☐, ☐, ☐, ☐

32: ☐, ☐, ☐, ☐, ☐, ☐

Common factors: ☐, ☐, ☐

Greatest common factor: ☐

24: ☐, ☐, ☐, ☐, ☐, ☐, ☐, ☐

60: ☐, ☐, ☐, ☐, ☐, ☐, ☐, ☐, ☐, ☐, ☐, ☐

Common factors: ☐, ☐, ☐, ☐, ☐

Greatest common factor: ☐

14

Unit Rewind

MULTIPLY each number by the first number, and WRITE the missing numbers in each pattern.

1.

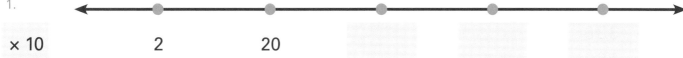

× 10   2   20

2.

× 6   3   18

3.

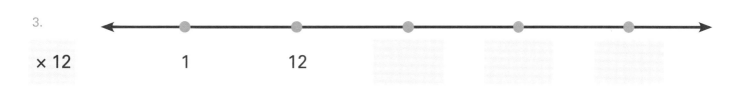

× 12   1   12

4.

× 15   4   60

Unit Rewind

ESTIMATE each product by rounding to the first digit and multiplying. WRITE the actual product to see how close your estimate was.

1.
```
    336
×   189
```
× _____

2.
```
    623
×   798
```
× _____

3.
```
  5,890
×   263
```
× _____

4.
```
  4,255
×   677
```
× _____

WRITE the factors of these numbers followed by the common factors and the greatest common factor.

18: ☐ , ☐ , ☐ , ☐ , ☐ , ☐

45: ☐ , ☐ , ☐ , ☐ , ☐ , ☐

Common factors: ☐ , ☐ , ☐

Greatest common factor: ☐

Pattern Patch

DIVIDE each number by the first number, and WRITE the missing numbers in each pattern.

Example:

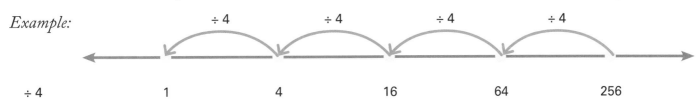

÷ 4   1   4   16   64   256

1.

÷ 2   1   16

2.

÷ 2   56   112

3.

÷ 3   27   81

4.

÷ 3   135   405

5.

÷ 5   1   625

Division Patterns

So Many Zeros

When one number (the **dividend**) is divided by another number (the **divisor**), the resulting number is called the **quotient**.

HINT: Try multiplying the quotient by the divisor to check your work.

Find the quotient of the first number in the dividend and divisor.

Next, subtract the number of zeros in the divisor from the number of zeros in the divided.

Write the difference of zeros after the quotient of the first numbers.

$$9,000 \div 30 = \underline{\quad}$$
$$9 \div 3 = 3$$
$$9,000 \div 30 = \underline{\quad}$$
$$9,000 \div 30 = 300$$

$$9 \div 3 = 3$$
$$90 \div 3 = 30$$
$$900 \div 30 = 30$$
$$9,000 \div 30 = 300$$
$$90,000 \div 300 = 300$$
$$900,000 \div 300 = 3,000$$

WRITE the quotients.

1.
$$8 \div 2 = \underline{\qquad}$$
$$80 \div 2 = \underline{\qquad}$$
$$800 \div 20 = \underline{\qquad}$$
$$8,000 \div 20 = \underline{\qquad}$$
$$80,000 \div 200 = \underline{\qquad}$$
$$800,000 \div 200 = \underline{\qquad}$$

2.
$$12 \div 4 = \underline{\qquad}$$
$$120 \div 4 = \underline{\qquad}$$
$$1,200 \div 40 = \underline{\qquad}$$
$$12,000 \div 40 = \underline{\qquad}$$
$$120,000 \div 400 = \underline{\qquad}$$
$$1,200,000 \div 400 = \underline{\qquad}$$

3.
$$10 \div 5 = \underline{\qquad}$$
$$100 \div 5 = \underline{\qquad}$$
$$1,000 \div 50 = \underline{\qquad}$$
$$10,000 \div 50 = \underline{\qquad}$$
$$100,000 \div 500 = \underline{\qquad}$$
$$1,000,000 \div 500 = \underline{\qquad}$$

4.
$$63 \div 7 = \underline{\qquad}$$
$$630 \div 7 = \underline{\qquad}$$
$$6,300 \div 70 = \underline{\qquad}$$
$$63,000 \div 70 = \underline{\qquad}$$
$$630,000 \div 700 = \underline{\qquad}$$
$$6,300,000 \div 700 = \underline{\qquad}$$

Computation Station

Divide a four-digit number by a one-digit number.

$8\overline{)6{,}048}$	$\begin{array}{r}7\\8\overline{)6{,}048}\\56\end{array}$	$\begin{array}{r}7\\8\overline{)6{,}048}\\-56\\\hline44\end{array}$	$\begin{array}{r}75\\8\overline{)6{,}048}\\-56\\\hline44\\40\end{array}$	$\begin{array}{r}75\\8\overline{)6{,}048}\\-56\\\hline44\\-40\\\hline48\end{array}$	$\begin{array}{r}756\\8\overline{)6{,}048}\\-56\\\hline44\\-40\\\hline48\\-48\\\hline0\end{array}$
6 cannot be divided by 8, so look to the next digit. Think of a multiple of 8 that is near 60 but not greater than 60.	$8 \times 7 = 56$	Subtract 56 from 60. Bring 4 down next to the 4.	Now divide 44 by 8. $8 \times 5 = 40$	Subtract and bring down the 8.	Divide 48 by 8.

WRITE each quotient.

1. $3\overline{)105}$

2. $7\overline{)413}$

3. $4\overline{)388}$

4. $6\overline{)114}$

5. $8\overline{)4{,}480}$

6. $2\overline{)1{,}838}$

7. $9\overline{)3{,}429}$

8. $3\overline{)2{,}262}$

9. $5\overline{)40{,}355}$

10. $4\overline{)29{,}372}$

11. $7\overline{)11{,}536}$

12. $8\overline{)36{,}736}$

Multidigit Division

Last Number Standing

Sometimes a number is not divided evenly. A number left over that is smaller than the divisor is called the **remainder**.

$7\overline{)3{,}755}$	$\begin{array}{r} 5 \\ 7\overline{)3{,}755} \\ -35 \\ \hline 2 \end{array}$	$\begin{array}{r} 53 \\ 7\overline{)3{,}755} \\ -35 \\ \hline 25 \\ -21 \\ \hline 4 \end{array}$	$\begin{array}{r} 536 \\ 7\overline{)3{,}755} \\ -35 \\ \hline 25 \\ -21 \\ \hline 45 \\ -42 \\ \hline ③ \end{array}$	$\begin{array}{r} 536\ \text{r3} \\ 7\overline{)3{,}755} \\ -35 \\ \hline 25 \\ -21 \\ \hline 45 \\ -42 \\ \hline 3 \end{array}$
			3 cannot be divided by 7. It is the remainder.	The answer is written as 536 r3.

WRITE each quotient.

1. $8\overline{)649}$

2. $3\overline{)236}$

3. $2\overline{)117}$

4. $5\overline{)474}$

5. $6\overline{)3{,}227}$

6. $4\overline{)1{,}375}$

7. $7\overline{)5{,}613}$

8. $8\overline{)2{,}873}$

9. $7\overline{)68{,}576}$

10. $8\overline{)51{,}323}$

11. $5\overline{)43{,}871}$

12. $9\overline{)14{,}659}$

Computation Station

WRITE each quotient.

HINT: Try writing multiples of the divisor before you begin.

$$17\overline{)638}$$

$$\begin{array}{r} 3 \\ 17\overline{)638} \\ -51 \\ \hline 12 \end{array}$$

$$\begin{array}{r} 37 \\ 17\overline{)638} \\ -51 \\ \hline 128 \\ -119 \\ \hline 9 \end{array}$$

$$\begin{array}{r} 37\ r9 \\ 17\overline{)638} \\ -51 \\ \hline 128 \\ -119 \\ \hline 9 \end{array}$$

1. $13\overline{)572}$

2. $39\overline{)663}$

3. $34\overline{)748}$

4. $21\overline{)819}$

5. $62\overline{)932}$

6. $12\overline{)853}$

7. $17\overline{)365}$

8. $24\overline{)646}$

9. $26\overline{)889}$

10. $55\overline{)774}$

11. $33\overline{)917}$

12. $45\overline{)599}$

Multidigit Division

Computation Station

WRITE each quotient.

```
                    2            21            217           217 r4
25)5,429    25)5,429    25)5,429    25)5,429    25)5,429
               -50          -50          -50          -50
                 4           42           42           42
                            -25          -25          -25
                             17          179          179
                                        -175         -175
                                           4            4
```

1. 20)3,540

2. 16)7,776

3. 43)4,859

4. 32)6,784

5. 41)9,268

6. 23)6,997

7. 54)9,944

8. 19)8,079

9. 24)7,827

10. 13)1,761

11. 33)6,414

12. 27)9,920

Computation Station

WRITE each quotient.

	1	1,7	1,70	1,707	1,707 r11
46)78,533	46)78,533	46)78,533	46)78,533	46)78,533	46)78,533
	−46	−46	−46	−46	−46
	32	325	325	325	325
		−322	−322	−322	−322
		3	33	33	33
			−0	−0	−0
			33	333	333
				−322	−322
				11	11

1. 30)38,430

2. 14)23,618

3. 22)50,952

4. 39)49,257

5. 28)96,938

6. 42)67,124

7. 51)52,502

8. 18)15,346

9. 12)28,783

10. 33)46,352

11. 74)87,651

12. 55)78,993

Multidigit Division

Safe Speeds

WRITE the answers.

HINT: Divide the number of miles by the number of hours.

If a car always travels at the same speed, how many miles per hour is it traveling?

1. 60 miles in 2 hours = _____30_____ miles per hour

2. 132 miles in 3 hours = _____ miles per hour

3. 435 miles in 15 hours = _____ miles per hour

4. 576 miles in 24 hours = _____ miles per hour

5. 1,040 miles in 20 hours = _____ miles per hour

6. 1,098 miles in 18 hours = _____ miles per hour

7. 1,344 miles in 32 hours = _____ miles per hour

8. 2,688 miles in 48 hours = _____ miles per hour

9. 3,575 miles in 65 hours = _____ miles per hour

10. 5,785 miles in 89 hours = _____ miles per hour

11. 5,278 miles in 91 hours = _____ miles per hour

12. 3,663 miles in 99 hours = _____ miles per hour

Rounding Estimates

Rounding numbers can help you estimate a quotient. With division, think about how you can round the dividend and divisor to make a problem that you can do in your head.

4,264 ÷ 13 =	To estimate, think about basic division facts. You know 45 ÷ 15 = 3, so estimate this problem by rounding the dividend to 4,500 and the divisor to 15. 4,500 ÷ 15 = 300 The answer is around 300. 4,264 ÷ 13 = 328
4,792 ÷ 63 =	48 ÷ 6 = 8 4,800 ÷ 60 = 80 The answer is around 80. 4792 ÷ 63 = 76 r4

ESTIMATE each quotient by rounding and then dividing. WRITE the actual quotient to check your estimate.

1. $5\overline{)97}$ ＿＿＿ ÷ ＿＿＿ = ＿＿＿＿

2. $6\overline{)5,415}$ ＿＿＿ ÷ ＿＿＿ = ＿＿＿＿

3. $11\overline{)408}$ ＿＿＿ ÷ ＿＿＿ = ＿＿＿＿

4. $67\overline{)2,079}$ ＿＿＿ ÷ ＿＿＿ = ＿＿＿＿

5. $82\overline{)55,691}$ ＿＿＿ ÷ ＿＿＿ = ＿＿＿＿

6. $29\overline{)91,101}$ ＿＿＿ ÷ ＿＿＿ = ＿＿＿＿

The Mighty Marlock

The Mighty Marlock will guess any quotient, but he sometimes guesses incorrectly.
ESTIMATE each quotient, and CROSS OUT any quotient that is clearly wrong.

827 ÷ 4 = 206 r3

75,733 ÷ 26 = 2,912 r21

637 ÷ 88 = 45 r2

4,954 ÷ 51 = 212 r6

12,275 ÷ 38 = 4,323 r1

3,569 ÷ 9 = 396 r5

Pathfinder

A **prime number** can only be divided evenly by itself and one. A **composite number** has more factors than itself and one.

Example: 13 is a prime number. The only factors of 13 are 1 and 13.
12 is a composite number. The factors of 12 are 1, 2, 3, 4, 6, and 12.

BEGIN at Start. FOLLOW the arrows. When you get to a box with two arrows, CHOOSE the box with a prime number. If you make all the right choices, you'll end up at Finish.

```
Start
  ↓
  7  →  19  →  10  →  24
  ↓      ↓      ↓      ↓
 16  ←  23  →   2  →  36
  ↓      ↑      ↓      ↓
 54  →  63  ←  11  ←   8
  ↑      ↑      ↓      ↓
  3  ←  29  ←   5  →  52
  ↓             ↑
 17  →  43  →  14  →  28
  ↓      ↓      ↑      ↓
 45  ←  13  →  61  →  Finish
```

Tic-Tac-Toe

CIRCLE each composite number. PUT an X through any prime number. DRAW a line when you find three composite numbers in a row. The line can go across, down, or diagonally.

Example:

(27)	(81)	X (13)
X (33)	(12)	(25)
2	(40)	X (47)

9	16	21
50	53	17
11	18	3

68	23	10
7	37	54
59	14	32

2	72	48
41	35	13
12	67	81

71	28	29
85	6	15
5	19	70

Unit Rewind

DIVIDE each number by the first number, and WRITE the missing numbers in each pattern.

1.

$\div 7$ 2   4,802

2.

$\div 11$ 5   73,205

WRITE each quotient.

3. $15\overline{)547}$ 4. $21\overline{)9,624}$ 5. $38\overline{)43,969}$ 6. $25\overline{)76,581}$

Unit Rewind

ESTIMATE each quotient by rounding and dividing. WRITE the actual quotient to check your estimate.

1. $72\overline{)3,530}$ _____ ÷ _____ = _____   2. $23\overline{)47,897}$ _____ ÷ _____ = _____

3. CIRCLE the prime numbers.

| 29 | 4 | 7 | 12 | 68 | 31 |

| 13 | 5 | 36 | 71 | 19 | 40 |

4. CIRCLE the composite numbers.

| 18 | 11 | 54 | 5 | 73 | 82 |

| 17 | 35 | 66 | 20 | 2 | 72 |

Find Your Place

A **decimal point** separates the part of the number that is one or greater than one from the part of the number that is less than one. IDENTIFY the place of each digit. Then WRITE the digit.

Example:

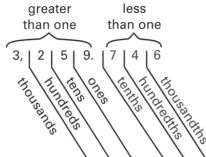

1. **7,361.248**

   7 thousands

   ___ hundreds

   ___ tens

   ___ ones

   ___ tenths

   ___ hundredths

   ___ thousandths

2. **9,482.156**

   ___ thousands

   ___ hundreds

   ___ tens

   ___ ones

   ___ tenths

   ___ hundredths

   ___ thousandths

3. **3,024.817**

   ___ thousands

   ___ hundreds

   ___ tens

   ___ ones

   ___ tenths

   ___ hundredths

   ___ thousandths

4. **8,210.539**

   ___ thousands

   ___ hundreds

   ___ tens

   ___ ones

   ___ tenths

   ___ hundredths

   ___ thousandths

5. **4,194.682**

   ___ thousands

   ___ hundreds

   ___ tens

   ___ ones

   ___ tenths

   ___ hundredths

   ___ thousandths

6. **1,576.041**

   ___ thousands

   ___ hundreds

   ___ tens

   ___ ones

   ___ tenths

   ___ hundredths

   ___ thousandths

High Fives

FIND the 5 in each number. WRITE the place of each 5.

1. 9,529.697   _____ place

2. 6,339.548   _____ place

3. 3,068.195   _____ place

4. 7,915.403   _____ place

5. 5,209.821   _____ place

6. 8,344.254   _____ place

7. 2,653.717   _____ place

8. 1,994.576   _____ place

9. 4,587.014   _____ place

10. 6,772.825   _____ place

Getting Bigger

Line up decimals when comparing numbers, and look at the size of the numbers of each place working left to right.

Example:

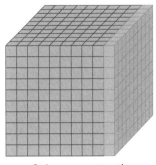
0.1 or one tenth

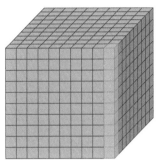
0.01 or one hundredth

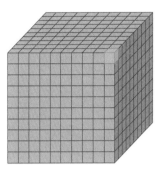
0.001 or one thousandth

0.1 is bigger than 0.01, which is bigger than 0.001.

WRITE the numbers from smallest to biggest.

1. 5.279   4.914
   4.914   4.952
   5.836   5.279
   4.952   5.836

2. 7.156 ____
   8.442 ____
   7.159 ____
   7.671 ____

3. 0.694 ____
   0.617 ____
   0.482 ____
   0.533 ____

4. 1.208 ____
   1.265 ____
   1.228 ____
   1.232 ____

5. 4.006 ____
   4.014 ____
   4.053 ____
   4.003 ____

6. 0.932 ____
   0.322 ____
   0.329 ____
   0.239 ____

Round About

Rounding makes numbers easier to work with.

Numbers that end in 0.001 through 0.499 get rounded **down** to the nearest one.

Numbers that end in 0.5 through 0.999 get rounded **up** to the nearest one.

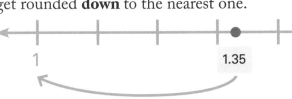
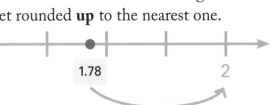

ROUND each number to the nearest one.

1. 1.2 _____
2. 8.6 _____
3. 6.1 _____
4. 3.7 _____
5. 4.9 _____
6. 3.5 _____
7. 5.4 _____
8. 9.8 _____
9. 2.63 _____
10. 9.24 _____
11. 0.47 _____
12. 7.96 _____
13. 6.104 _____
14. 2.859 _____
15. 0.621 _____
16. 7.482 _____

Cash Crunch

WRITE the decimal for each picture. Then ROUND to the nearest dollar.

1.

   $ <u>11.79</u> $ <u>12.00</u>

2.

   $ _____ $ _____

3.

   $ _____ $ _____

4.

   $ _____ $ _____

5.

   $ _____ $ _____

6.

   $ _____ $ _____

Round About

When rounding, look at the digit to the right of the place you're rounding to. If that digit is less than 5, round down. If it is 5 or greater, round up.

Example:

3.43 rounded to the nearest tenth is 3.4.

3.48 rounded to the nearest tenth is 3.5.

7.282 rounded to the nearest hundredth is 7.28.

7.286 rounded to the nearest hundredth is 7.29.

ROUND each number to the nearest tenth.

1. 2.23 _____

2. 5.67 _____

3. 8.18 _____

4. 1.84 _____

5. 3.29 _____

6. 7.71 _____

7. 4.05 _____

8. 0.02 _____

ROUND each number to the nearest hundredth.

9. 9.549 _____

10. 4.477 _____

11. 1.915 _____

12. 4.534 _____

13. 2.382 _____

14. 5.174 _____

15. 3.086 _____

16. 6.903 _____

Rather Rounded

ROUND each number to the nearest one, tenth, and hundredth.

	Nearest One	Nearest Tenth	Nearest Hundredth
25.158	25	25.2	25.16
1.372			
83.614			
390.293			
7.872			
14.426			
5.555			
0.307			

Cash Crunch

ADD or SUBTRACT the dollar amounts.

Example: $21.25
              + 5.62
              ———
              $26.87

1. $ 7.14
    +   2.62
    ————
    $

2. $ 20.03
    +   9.52
    ————
    $

3. $ 56.31
    + 31.17
    ————
    $

4. $ 34.02
    + 24.23
    ————
    $

5. $171.66
    + 18.21
    ————
    $

6. $521.40
    +454.23
    ————
    $

7. $ 8.79
    –   3.48
    ————
    $

8. $ 64.29
    –   2.06
    ————
    $

9. $ 56.97
    – 11.95
    ————
    $

10. $ 37.47
    – 13.03
    ————
    $

11. $584.97
    – 73.07
    ————
    $

12. $668.88
    –431.31
    ————
    $

Adding & Subtracting Decimals

It All Adds Up

When adding decimals, add and regroup as you normally would, keeping the decimal between the ones place and the tenths place.

36.274 + 18.85 _____ 4	¹ 36.274 + 18.85 _____ 24	¹ ¹ 36.274 + 18.85 _____ .124	¹ ¹ ¹ 36.274 + 18.85 _____ 5.124	¹ ¹ ¹ 36.274 + 18.85 _____ 55.124
Add the thousandths. Think of this as 4 + 0 = 4.	Add the hundredths. 7 + 5 = 12	Add the tenths. 1 + 2 + 8 = 11	Add the ones. 1 + 6 + 8 = 15	Add the tens. 1 + 3 + 1 = 5

WRITE the sum.

1.
```
    6.7
+   2.8
```

2.
```
    8.92
+   2.7
```

3.
```
  36.35
+  4.49
```

4.
```
   52.9
+ 34.12
```

5.
```
  48.28
+ 60.27
```

6.
```
  91.257
+ 14.13
```

7.
```
  121.98
+  29.577
```

8.
```
  455.91
+ 219.40
```

9.
```
  779.04
+ 587.8
```

10.
```
  494.292
+ 244.07
```

11.
```
  2,717.152
+   213.23
```

12.
```
  8,212.67
+ 1,831.75
```

What's the Difference?

When subtracting decimals, subtract and regroup as you normally would, keeping the decimal between the ones place and the tenths place.

$\overset{5\ 17}{441.\cancel{6}\cancel{7}}$	$\overset{5\ 17}{441.\cancel{6}\cancel{7}}$	$\overset{3\ 11\ \ 5\ 17}{44\cancel{1}.\cancel{6}\cancel{7}}$	$\overset{3\ 13\ 11\ \ 5\ 17}{\cancel{4}\cancel{4}\cancel{1}.\cancel{6}\cancel{7}}$	$\overset{3\ 13\ 11\ \ 5\ 17}{\cancel{4}\cancel{4}\cancel{1}.\cancel{6}\cancel{7}}$
$-\ 262.49$	$-\ 262.49$	$-\ 262.49$	$-\ 262.49$	$-\ 262.49$
$\overline{8}$	$\overline{18}$	$\overline{9.18}$	$\overline{79.18}$	$\overline{179.18}$
Subtract the hundredths. $17 - 9 = 8$	Subtract the tenths. $5 - 4 = 1$	Subtract the ones. $11 - 2 = 9$	Subtract the tens. $13 - 6 = 7$	Subtract the hundreds. $3 - 2 = 1$

WRITE each difference.

1.
$$\begin{array}{r} 8.2 \\ -\ 4.8 \\ \hline \end{array}$$

2.
$$\begin{array}{r} 9.83 \\ -\ 7.05 \\ \hline \end{array}$$

3.
$$\begin{array}{r} 60.26 \\ -\ 1.3 \\ \hline \end{array}$$

4.
$$\begin{array}{r} 46.491 \\ -\ 28.56 \\ \hline \end{array}$$

5.
$$\begin{array}{r} 79.5 \\ -\ 30.99 \\ \hline \end{array}$$

6.
$$\begin{array}{r} 550.21 \\ -\ 14.74 \\ \hline \end{array}$$

7.
$$\begin{array}{r} 962.97 \\ -\ 208.6 \\ \hline \end{array}$$

8.
$$\begin{array}{r} 163.469 \\ -\ 135.82 \\ \hline \end{array}$$

9.
$$\begin{array}{r} 795.18 \\ -\ 323.62 \\ \hline \end{array}$$

10.
$$\begin{array}{r} 877.188 \\ -\ 293.94 \\ \hline \end{array}$$

11.
$$\begin{array}{r} 4,445.53 \\ -\ 2,465.75 \\ \hline \end{array}$$

12.
$$\begin{array}{r} 9,020.9 \\ -\ 1,252.75 \\ \hline \end{array}$$

Round About

Rounding numbers can help you estimate a sum or difference.

$$\begin{array}{r} 5.9\,3 \\ -2.1\,6 \\ \hline \end{array} \quad \longrightarrow \quad \begin{array}{r} 6 \\ -\,2 \\ \hline 4 \end{array}$$

5.93 rounded to the nearest one is 6.
2.16 rounded to the nearest one is 2.
$6 - 2 = 4$
$5.93 - 2.16 = 3.77$

ESTIMATE each answer by rounding to the first digit and and then adding or subtracting. WRITE the actual sum or difference to check your estimate.

1.
$$\begin{array}{r} 3.42 \\ +\,5.6 \\ \hline \end{array} \qquad \begin{array}{r} \\ + \\ \hline \end{array}$$

2.
$$\begin{array}{r} 1.84 \\ +\,4.95 \\ \hline \end{array} \qquad \begin{array}{r} \\ + \\ \hline \end{array}$$

3.
$$\begin{array}{r} 4.068 \\ +\,6.75 \\ \hline \end{array} \qquad \begin{array}{r} \\ + \\ \hline \end{array}$$

4.
$$\begin{array}{r} 6.17 \\ -\,2.9 \\ \hline \end{array} \qquad \begin{array}{r} \\ - \\ \hline \end{array}$$

5.
$$\begin{array}{r} 9.81 \\ -\,5.66 \\ \hline \end{array} \qquad \begin{array}{r} \\ - \\ \hline \end{array}$$

6.
$$\begin{array}{r} 12.691 \\ -\,4.32 \\ \hline \end{array} \qquad \begin{array}{r} \\ - \\ \hline \end{array}$$

Computation Station

When multiplying decimals, you do not need to line up the decimal points. When writing the product, count how many digits there are to the right of the decimal points in the factors. Then count that many places from the right in the product, and insert the decimal point.

```
  4 1            1
  4.5 2          4.5 2              4.5 2                    4.5 2
×    3.9       ×    3.9          ×     3.9               ×     3.9
  4 0 6 8        4 0 6 8            4 0 6 8                  4 0 6 8
              1 3 5 6 0        + 1 3 5 6 0              + 1 3 5 6 0
                                 1 7 6 2 8                 1 7.6 2 8
```

Solve the problem the same way you would if there were no decimal points.

In the factors, there are a total of three digits to the right of the decimal. Put a decimal point in the product three places from the right.

WRITE each product.

1.
```
    1.9
×     7
```

2.
```
    7.3
×     5
```

3.
```
   8.6 3
×      3
```

4.
```
    2.7
×   4 6
```

5.
```
    9.6
× 2.2
```

6.
```
    6.7
× 8.4
```

7.
```
    5.1
× 3.8
```

8.
```
    7.5
× 1.3
```

9.
```
   3.8 3
×    4.9
```

10.
```
   1.7 6
×    0.2
```

11.
```
   8.1 6
×    5.4
```

12.
```
   9.2 2
×    6.5
```

Multiplying & Dividing Decimals

Computation Station

When dividing decimals, line up the decimal point in the quotient with the same place in the dividend.

$$
\begin{array}{r} \\ 21\overline{)7.476} \end{array}
\qquad
\begin{array}{r} 3 \\ 21\overline{)7.476} \\ -63 \\ \hline 11 \end{array}
\qquad
\begin{array}{r} 35 \\ 21\overline{)7.476} \\ -63 \\ \hline 117 \\ -105 \\ \hline 12 \end{array}
\qquad
\begin{array}{r} 356 \\ 21\overline{)7.476} \\ -63 \\ \hline 117 \\ -105 \\ \hline 126 \\ -126 \\ \hline 0 \end{array}
\qquad
\begin{array}{r} 0.356 \\ 21\overline{)7.476} \\ -63 \\ \hline 117 \\ -105 \\ \hline 126 \\ -126 \\ \hline 0 \end{array}
$$

Solve the problem the same way you would if there were no decimal points.

Put a decimal point in the quotient aligned with the one in the dividend. If there is no digit to the left of the decimal point, add a zero.

WRITE each quotient.

1. $9\overline{)6.3}$

2. $6\overline{)2.4}$

3. $5\overline{)8.35}$

4. $3\overline{)9.81}$

5. $8\overline{)23.28}$

6. $4\overline{)17.28}$

7. $2\overline{)6.234}$

8. $4\overline{)2.296}$

9. $11\overline{)64.46}$

10. $25\overline{)86.25}$

11. $15\overline{)3.945}$

12. $41\overline{)7.134}$

Rounding Estimates

Rounding numbers can help you estimate a product or quotient.

$$\begin{array}{r} 8.\,8\ 4 \\ \times\quad 7.\,3 \\ \hline \end{array} \quad\longrightarrow\quad \begin{array}{r} 9 \\ \times\ 7 \\ \hline 6\ 3 \end{array}$$

8.84 rounded to the nearest one is 9.
7.3 rounded to the nearest one is 7.
$9 \times 7 = 63$
$8.84 \times 7.3 = 64.532$

$3.684 \div 12 =$	Look for a convenient way to round the numbers so that you can use basic facts. Think $36 \div 12 = 3$.	$3.600 \div 12 = 0.300$ The answer is around 0.3. $3.684 \div 12 = 0.307$

ROUND the numbers to estimate each product. WRITE the estimate.

1. 4.2×6.9

   _____ × _____ = _____

2. 3.8×3.8

   _____ × _____ = _____

3. 5.106×8.3

   _____ × _____ = _____

4. 2.94×40.3

   _____ × _____ = _____

5. 4.281×10.925

   _____ × _____ = _____

6. 9.237×8.886

   _____ × _____ = _____

ROUND the numbers to estimate each quotient. WRITE the estimate.

7. $5.9 \div 6$

   _____ ÷ _____ = _____

8. $4.9 \div 8$

   _____ ÷ _____ = _____

9. $9.288 \div 3$

   _____ ÷ _____ = _____

10. $1.244 \div 6$

    _____ ÷ _____ = _____

11. $4.462 \div 5$

    _____ ÷ _____ = _____

12. $109.78 \div 11$

    _____ ÷ _____ = _____

The Powers of Ten

Notice the movement of the decimal point as numbers are multiplied and divided by multiples of ten.

$3.514 \times 10 = 35.14$	$3.514 \rightarrow 35.14$	When multiplying by 10, move the decimal point one place to the right.
$3.514 \times 100 = 351.4$	$3.514 \rightarrow 351.4$	When multiplying by 100, move the decimal point two places to the right.
$3.514 \times 1000 = 3514$	$3.514 \rightarrow 3,514$	When multiplying by 1,000, move the decimal point three places to the right.
$3514 \div 10 = 351.4$	$3514 \rightarrow 351.4$	When dividing by 10, move the decimal point one place to the left.
$3514 \div 100 = 35.14$	$3514 \rightarrow 35.14$	When dividing by 100, move the decimal point two places to the left.
$3514 \div 100 = 3.514$	$3514 \rightarrow 3.514$	When dividing by 1,000, move the decimal point three places to the left.

WRITE each product.

1. $4.51 \times 10 =$ _____

2. $1.983 \times 10 =$ _____

3. $7.242 \times 100 =$ _____

4. $0.603 \times 100 =$ _____

5. $8.599 \times 1,000 =$ _____

6. $4.217 \times 1,000 =$ _____

WRITE each quotient.

7. $3.6 \div 10 =$ _____

8. $77.38 \div 10 =$ _____

9. $936.6 \div 100 =$ _____

10. $54,103 \div 100 =$ _____

11. $38,249 \div 1,000 =$ _____

12. $572 \div 1,000 =$ _____

Unit Rewind

WRITE >, <, or = in the box.

5.58 ☐ 4.3	6.35 ☐ 6.5	9.82 ☐ 9.82	2.71 ☐ 3.01	0.16 ☐ 0.09
1	2	3	4	5

7.588 ☐ 7.32	1.596 ☐ 1.65	4.518 ☐ 4.521	3.762 ☐ 3.762	7.173 ☐ 7.174
6	7	8	9	10

ROUND each number to the nearest one.

11. 5.2 _____   12. 9.41 _____   13. 34.73 _____   14. 0.55 _____

ROUND each number to the nearest tenth.

15. 6.63 _____   16. 25.87 _____   17. 0.759 _____   18. 7.644 _____

ROUND each number to the nearest hundredth.

19. 5.984 _____   20. 0.158 _____   21. 5.905 _____   22. 0.006 _____

Unit Rewind

ESTIMATE the answer to each problem.

1. $3.2 + 7.8 =$ _____

2. $8.6 - 1.9 =$ _____

3. $5.9 \times 2.3 =$ _____

4. $8.3 \div 9 =$ _____

5. $4.561 + 4.42 =$ _____

6. $20.35 - 7.677 =$ _____

7. $7.208 \times 9.594 =$ _____

8. $98.978 \div 20 =$ _____

WRITE the answer to each problem.

9.
$$\begin{array}{r} 30.54 \\ +7.39 \\ \hline \end{array}$$

10.
$$\begin{array}{r} 648.41 \\ -25.32 \\ \hline \end{array}$$

11.
$$\begin{array}{r} 2.929 \\ \times6 \\ \hline \end{array}$$

12.
$$5\overline{)12.05}$$

13.
$$\begin{array}{r} 825.67 \\ +199.53 \\ \hline \end{array}$$

14.
$$\begin{array}{r} 230.608 \\ -55.442 \\ \hline \end{array}$$

15.
$$\begin{array}{r} 76.35 \\ \times18.9 \\ \hline \end{array}$$

16.
$$13\overline{)6.773}$$

17. $78.2 \times 10 =$ _____

18. $0.345 \times 1{,}000 =$ _____

19. $44{,}982 \div 100 =$ _____

20. $9{,}200 \div 1{,}000 =$ _____

Any Way You Slice It

WRITE the fraction for each picture.

Example: $\dfrac{4}{9}$ ← The **numerator** represents the number of shaded sections.

← The **denominator** represents the total number of sections.

 ____

1

 ____

2

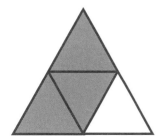 ____

3

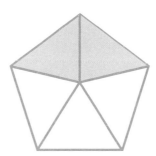 ____

4

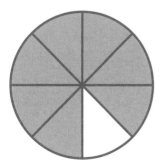 ____

5

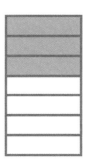 ____

6

7. Which two fractions have the same numerator? ____ ____

8. Which two fractions have the same denominator? ____ ____

Numerators & Denominators

Color Sets

COLOR each set of shapes to match the fraction.

Example:

$\dfrac{3}{}$ ← The **numerator** represents the number of colored objects.

$\dfrac{}{5}$ ← The **denominator** represents the total number of objects.

1. $\dfrac{2}{9}$

2. $\dfrac{5}{6}$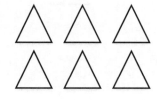

3. $\dfrac{4}{7}$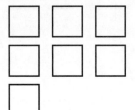

4. $\dfrac{3}{10}$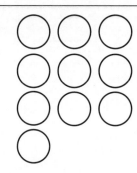

5. $\dfrac{6}{7}$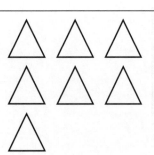

6. $\dfrac{2}{5}$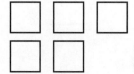

7. Which two fractions have the same numerator? —— ——

8. Which two fractions have the same denominator? —— ——

50

Circle the Same

Equivalent fractions are fractions that have the same value.

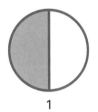  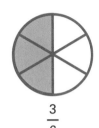

These fractions are different, but the same amount is shaded.

They are equivalent: All are equal to $\frac{1}{2}$ of the circle.

$\frac{1}{2}$ $\qquad$ $\frac{2}{4}$ $\qquad$ $\frac{3}{6}$

CIRCLE the fraction in each row that is equivalent to the first fraction.

1.  $\frac{1}{3}$ $\qquad$  $\frac{2}{4}$ $\qquad$ 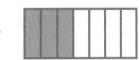 $\frac{3}{7}$ $\qquad$  $\frac{3}{9}$

2.  $\frac{9}{12}$ $\qquad$  $\frac{4}{7}$ $\qquad$  $\frac{3}{4}$ $\qquad$  $\frac{4}{6}$

3. 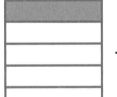 $\frac{1}{5}$ $\qquad$ 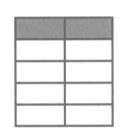 $\frac{2}{10}$ $\qquad$  $\frac{3}{9}$ $\qquad$ 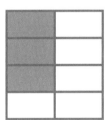 $\frac{3}{8}$

4.  $\frac{2}{6}$ $\qquad$ $\frac{2}{7}$ $\qquad$  $\frac{1}{3}$ $\qquad$ 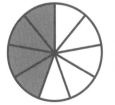 $\frac{4}{9}$

Equivalent Fractions

Slicing and Dicing

WRITE the numerator to make a fraction equivalent to the first fraction. Then COLOR the pictures to match the fractions.

HINT: When you color the fractions, they should show the same shaded amount.

Example: $\dfrac{1}{2}$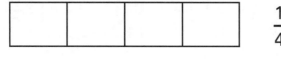

$\dfrac{2}{4}$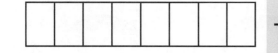

If you multiply the same number to the numerator and denominator, the new fraction will be equivalent.

$\dfrac{1}{2} \times \dfrac{2}{2} = \dfrac{2}{4}$ $\dfrac{1}{2}$ is equivalent to $\dfrac{2}{4}$.

1.

$\dfrac{1}{4}$

$\dfrac{}{8}$

2.
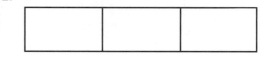
$\dfrac{2}{3}$

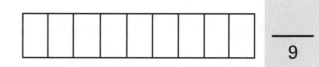
$\dfrac{}{9}$

3.
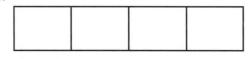
$\dfrac{3}{4}$

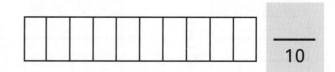
$\dfrac{}{12}$

4.
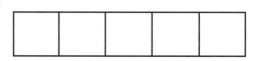
$\dfrac{2}{5}$

$\dfrac{}{10}$

5.
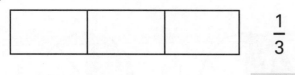
$\dfrac{1}{3}$

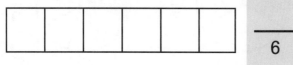
$\dfrac{}{6}$

6.
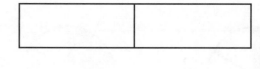
$\dfrac{1}{2}$

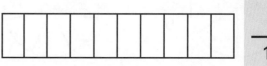
$\dfrac{}{10}$

Slicing and Dicing

A fraction is in its **simplest form** if the only common factor of the numerator and the denominator is 1.

Example: $\frac{8}{12}$  The common factors of 8 and 12 are 1, 2, and 4. Divide the numerator and the denominator by the greatest common factor, 4.

$\frac{2}{3}$ $\frac{8 \div 4}{12 \div 4} = \frac{2}{3}$ The simplest form of $\frac{8}{12}$ is $\frac{2}{3}$.

The only common factor of 2 and 3 is 1.

WRITE the fraction in its simplest form. Then COLOR the pictures to match the fractions.

HINT: When you color the fractions, they should show the same shaded amount.

1.

$\frac{3}{9}$

——

2.
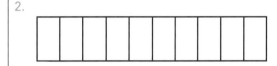
$\frac{2}{10}$

——

3.

$\frac{4}{12}$

——

4.

$\frac{6}{8}$

——

5.
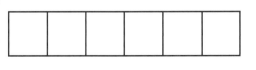
$\frac{3}{6}$

——

6.
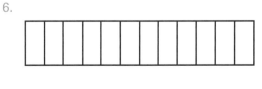
$\frac{2}{12}$

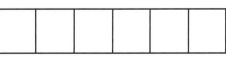
——

Simplifying Fractions

Simply Simplify

WRITE each fraction in its simplest form.

1. $\dfrac{4}{6}$ ___

2. $\dfrac{9}{18}$ ___

3. $\dfrac{5}{15}$ ___

4. $\dfrac{2}{8}$ ___

5. $\dfrac{8}{20}$ ___

6. $\dfrac{12}{16}$ ___

7. $\dfrac{10}{12}$ ___

8. $\dfrac{20}{45}$ ___

9. $\dfrac{28}{32}$ ___

10. $\dfrac{24}{40}$ ___

11. $\dfrac{36}{63}$ ___

12. $\dfrac{72}{80}$ ___

Prim and Proper

An **improper fraction** is a fraction with a numerator larger than its denominator. The simplest form of an improper fraction is called a **mixed number**. WRITE the mixed number for each fraction.

Example:

$$\frac{8}{5} = 1\frac{3}{5}$$

$$\frac{5}{5} = 1 \qquad \frac{3}{5}$$

$$\frac{13}{7}$$

1

$$\frac{9}{4}$$

2

$$\frac{13}{9}$$

3

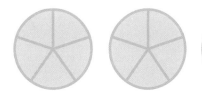

$$\frac{12}{5}$$

4

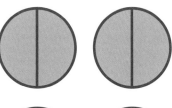

$$\frac{7}{2}$$

5

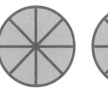

$$\frac{29}{8}$$

6

Mix Masters

WRITE the mixed number for each fraction.

To find the mixed number, think of $\frac{31}{5}$ as a way of saying $31 \div 5$.

$$5\overline{)\begin{array}{r} 6\,r1 \\ 3\,1 \\ -\,3\,0 \\ \hline 1 \end{array}}$$

$$1 \div 5 = \frac{1}{5}$$

$$\frac{31}{5} = 6\,r1 = 6\frac{1}{5}$$

1. $\frac{11}{4}$

2. $\frac{24}{5}$

3. $\frac{19}{3}$

4. $\frac{9}{2}$

5. $\frac{52}{7}$

6. $\frac{11}{10}$

7. $\frac{65}{6}$

8. $\frac{43}{8}$

9. $\frac{23}{3}$

10. $\frac{31}{9}$

11. $\frac{57}{5}$

12. $\frac{43}{12}$

Unmixed

When changing a mixed number into an improper fraction, the denominator stays the same. You need to find the numerator. WRITE the improper fraction for each mixed number.

$3\frac{4}{5}$	3 is like having $\frac{5}{5}$ three times, plus $\frac{4}{5}$ left over. Multiply 3 by 5. Then add the 4, which is in the numerator already. $3 \times 5 = 15$ $15 + 4 = 19$	The improper fraction for $3\frac{4}{5}$ is $\frac{19}{5}$.

1. $8\frac{1}{2}$ ____

2. $2\frac{1}{6}$ ____

3. $7\frac{3}{4}$ ____

4. $3\frac{2}{3}$ ____

5. $10\frac{2}{9}$ ____

6. $4\frac{1}{6}$ ____

7. $5\frac{3}{8}$ ____

8. $6\frac{2}{5}$ ____

9. $3\frac{1}{11}$ ____

10. $9\frac{1}{4}$ ____

11. $4\frac{4}{10}$ ____

12. $8\frac{7}{9}$ ____

Improper Fractions & Mixed Numbers

Odd One Out

CROSS OUT the fraction or mixed number in each row that is not equivalent.

1.

$2\frac{1}{5}$ $\frac{11}{5}$ $1\frac{2}{5}$ $\frac{22}{10}$

2.

$\frac{27}{8}$ $4\frac{1}{4}$ $\frac{17}{4}$ $4\frac{2}{8}$

3.

$\frac{5}{3}$ $\frac{10}{3}$ $1\frac{2}{3}$ $\frac{10}{6}$

4.

$2\frac{3}{10}$ $\frac{61}{10}$ $6\frac{1}{10}$ $\frac{610}{100}$

5.

$\frac{50}{7}$ $7\frac{1}{7}$ $\frac{100}{14}$ $7\frac{3}{7}$

6.

$\frac{24}{4}$ 6 $6\frac{3}{4}$ $\frac{12}{2}$

Tiny Tenths

This picture has $\frac{3}{10}$ shaded. In decimal form this is written as 0.3.

$\frac{3}{10}$ = 3 ÷ 10

3 ÷ 10 = 0.3   Remember, when dividing by 10, move the decimal to the left one place.

WRITE the fraction and decimal for each picture.

HINT: If the number is less than one, put a zero before the decimal point.

1.

___

2.

___

3.

___

4.

___

5.

___

6.

___

Handy Hundredths

This picture has $\frac{72}{100}$ shaded. In decimal form this is written as 0.72.

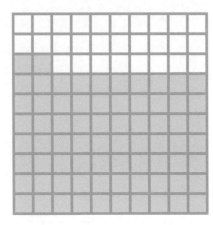

$$\frac{72}{100} = 72 \div 100$$

$$72 \div 100 = 0.72$$

Remember, when dividing by 100, move the decimal to the left two places.

WRITE the fraction and decimal for each picture.

1.
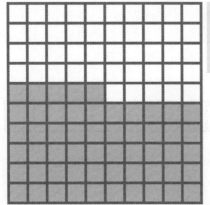

_____

2.
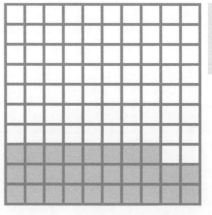

_____

3.
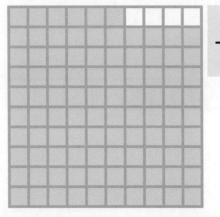

_____

4.
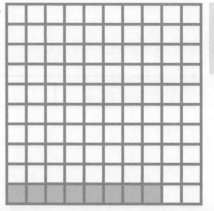

_____

Pictured Percent

A **percent** (%) is another way of showing parts of 100. The picture has $\frac{46}{100}$ shaded. It can also be written as 46%.

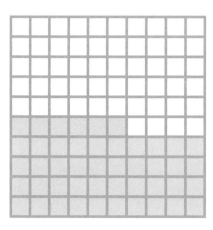

$$\frac{46}{100} = 46\%$$

WRITE the fraction and percent for each picture.

1. 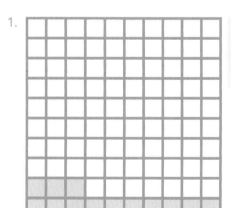 ———   ———

2. 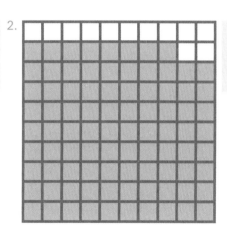 ———   ———

3. 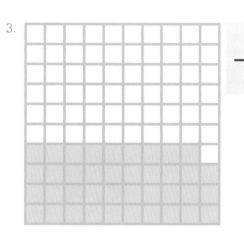 ———   ———

4. 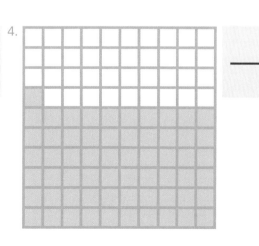 ———   ———

Paired Parts

WRITE each fraction as a percent and each percent as a fraction in its simplest form.

Examples:

$$\frac{4 \times 4 = 16}{25 \times 4 = 100} = 16\%$$ $$90\% = \frac{90 \div 10 = 9}{100 \div 10 = 10}$$

1. $\dfrac{6}{10}$ =

2. $\dfrac{16}{50}$ =

3. $\dfrac{1}{5}$ =

4. $\dfrac{1}{2}$ =

5. $\dfrac{12}{25}$ =

6. $\dfrac{3}{20}$ =

7. 14% = ——

8. 40% = ——

9. 36% = ——

10. 10% = ——

11. 35% = ——

12. 23% = ——

Write It

WRITE each decimal as a percent and each percent as a decimal.

HINT: Thinking about the equivalent fraction may help.

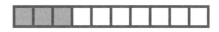

$$0.3 = \frac{3}{10} = \frac{30}{100} = 30\%$$

0.2 =

1

0.45 =

2

0.99 =

3

0.13 =

4

0.51 =

5

0.88 =

6

0.27 =

7

0.06 =

8

0.39 =

9

0.21 =

10

0.72 =

11

0.63 =

12

75% =

13

46% =

14

32% =

15

93% =

16

8% =

17

15% =

18

84% =

19

1% =

20

51% =

21

27% =

22

68% =

23

82% =

24

Fractions, Decimals & Percents

Pinpoint Percents

To find the percent of a number, change the percent to a decimal and multiply.

Example: 61% of 85 = 0.61 × 85 = 51.85

$$
\begin{array}{r}
\overset{3}{8\,5} \\
\times\ \ 0.6\,1 \\
\hline
8\,5 \\
+5\,1\,0\,0 \\
\hline
5\,1.8\,5
\end{array}
$$

WRITE the percent of each number.

75% of 48 =
1

30% of 70 =
2

25% of 52 =
3

50% of 15 =
4

6% of 91 =
5

40% of 84 =
6

16% of 22 =
7

95% of 37 =
8

87% of 5 =
9

Odd One Out

CROSS OUT the number or picture in each row that does **not** have the same value as the others.

1.   0.45 $\dfrac{1}{2}$ 50%

2.   75% $\dfrac{3}{4}$ 0.7

3.   30%   0.3    $\dfrac{3}{10}$

4.   0.10   100% $\dfrac{1}{10}$

5. $\dfrac{3}{8}$ [circle image]   25%   0.25

Matched or Mismatched?

WRITE >, <, or = in the box.

1. 50% ☐ $\dfrac{1}{2}$

2. 0.6 ☐ $\dfrac{3}{10}$

3. 32% ☐ 0.52

4. $\dfrac{22}{25}$ ☐ 75%

5. $\dfrac{9}{20}$ ☐ 0.98

6. 0.13 ☐ 12%

7. $\dfrac{39}{50}$ ☐ 82%

8. 0.8 ☐ $\dfrac{4}{5}$

9. 47% ☐ 0.39

10. 25% ☐ $\dfrac{4}{16}$

11. $\dfrac{6}{7}$ ☐ 0.6

12. 0.099 ☐ 99%

13. $\dfrac{3}{13}$ ☐ 31%

14. 0.26 ☐ $\dfrac{7}{25}$

15. 62% ☐ 0.62

16. 78% ☐ $\dfrac{24}{30}$

Unit Rewind

CIRCLE all of the fractions equivalent to $\frac{3}{5}$.

1.
$\frac{3}{6}$
$\frac{6}{10}$
$\frac{6}{5}$
$\frac{15}{25}$
$\frac{5}{3}$
$\frac{30}{50}$

WRITE each fraction in its simplest form.

$\frac{16}{32}$ ____

$\frac{35}{45}$ ____

$\frac{27}{90}$ ____

$\frac{60}{72}$ ____

2
3
4
5

WRITE the mixed number for each fraction.

$\frac{11}{5}$ ____

$\frac{65}{7}$ ____

$\frac{43}{10}$ ____

$\frac{29}{9}$ ____

6
7
8
9

WRITE the improper fraction for each mixed number.

$1\frac{5}{7}$ ____

$3\frac{5}{6}$ ____

$8\frac{1}{4}$ ____

$4\frac{2}{11}$ ____

10
11
12
13

Unit Rewind

WRITE percents, decimals, and fractions in their simplest form to make each row in the chart equivalent.

Percent	Decimal	Fraction
		$\dfrac{7}{10}$
20%		
	0.8	
35%		
		$\dfrac{33}{50}$
	0.04	

WRITE the percent of each number.

1. 26% of 60 = _____

2. 43% of 27 = _____

3. 99% of 94 = _____

Picture It

When fractions have the same denominator, add them by adding only the numerators. The denominator stays the same. ADD the fractions and WRITE the sum.

Example:

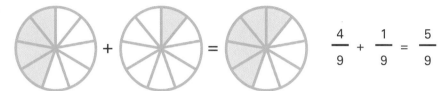

$$\frac{4}{9} + \frac{1}{9} = \frac{5}{9}$$

$$\frac{1}{5} + \frac{3}{5} = \underline{\hspace{2cm}}$$

1

$$\frac{3}{7} + \frac{3}{7} = \underline{\hspace{2cm}}$$

2

$$\frac{4}{11} + \frac{6}{11} = \underline{\hspace{2cm}}$$

3

$$\frac{5}{8} + \frac{3}{8} = \underline{\hspace{2cm}}$$

4

$$\frac{5}{14} + \frac{4}{14} = \underline{\hspace{2cm}}$$

5

Adding Fractions

Simplified Sums

WRITE each sum as a fraction in its simplest form.

Examples: $\dfrac{3}{15} + \dfrac{6}{15} = \dfrac{9}{15} = \dfrac{3}{5}$ $\dfrac{5}{6} + \dfrac{8}{6} = \dfrac{13}{6} = 2\dfrac{1}{6}$

$\dfrac{1}{3} + \dfrac{7}{3} =$

1

$\dfrac{3}{16} + \dfrac{5}{16} =$

2

$\dfrac{7}{9} + \dfrac{7}{9} =$

3

$\dfrac{4}{18} + \dfrac{11}{18} =$

4

$\dfrac{14}{8} + \dfrac{21}{8} =$

5

$\dfrac{5}{21} + \dfrac{9}{21} =$

6

$\dfrac{40}{7} + \dfrac{9}{7} =$

7

$\dfrac{27}{45} + \dfrac{8}{45} =$

8

$\dfrac{30}{12} + \dfrac{33}{12} =$

9

$\dfrac{14}{15} + \dfrac{10}{15} =$

10

Dueling Denominators

The **lowest common denominator** between two fractions is the smallest number that is a multiple of both denominators.

$$\frac{3}{4} + \frac{2}{3} =$$

Multiples of 4 are: 4, 8, **12**, 16, 20 . . .
Multiples of 3 are: 3, 6, 9, **12**, 15 . . .
12 is the least common multiple of 3 and 4, making it the lowest common denominator.

Multiply the numerator and denominator in each fraction by the number that will make the denominator 12. Then add the two numbers.

$$\frac{3 \times 3 = 9}{4 \times 3 = 12} \qquad \frac{2 \times 4 = 8}{3 \times 4 = 12}$$

$$\frac{9}{12} + \frac{8}{12} = \frac{17}{12} = 1\frac{5}{12}$$

REWRITE the fractions with their lowest common denominators. Then WRITE the sum as a fraction in its simplest form.

$$\frac{1}{2} + \frac{2}{3} =$$

1

$$\frac{2}{12} + \frac{1}{6} =$$

2

$$\frac{3}{2} + \frac{13}{8} =$$

3

$$\frac{2}{5} + \frac{3}{4} =$$

4

$$\frac{4}{3} + \frac{8}{9} =$$

5

$$\frac{9}{16} + \frac{7}{8} =$$

6

$$\frac{15}{18} + \frac{7}{6} =$$

7

$$\frac{8}{9} + \frac{5}{12} =$$

8

$$\frac{7}{6} + \frac{23}{24} =$$

9

Adding Fractions

Mixed Up

When adding mixed numbers, think of it as two whole numbers plus two fractions. Find the lowest common denominator to add the fractions.

Example: $2\dfrac{1}{6} + 7\dfrac{2}{3} =$

$$(2 + 7) + \left(\dfrac{1}{6} + \dfrac{2}{3}\right) = 9 + \left(\dfrac{1}{6} + \dfrac{4}{6}\right) = 9\dfrac{5}{6}$$

WRITE each sum as a fraction in its simplest form.

$1\dfrac{3}{7} + 6\dfrac{1}{7} =$

1

$4\dfrac{1}{2} + 2\dfrac{1}{8} =$

2

$3\dfrac{4}{5} + 5\dfrac{2}{15} =$

3

$7\dfrac{2}{3} + 2\dfrac{2}{9} =$

4

$2\dfrac{3}{10} + 1\dfrac{2}{5} =$

5

$3\dfrac{7}{12} + 3\dfrac{1}{4} =$

6

$5\dfrac{1}{9} + 3\dfrac{7}{18} =$

7

$7\dfrac{3}{4} + 4\dfrac{5}{8} =$

8

$6\dfrac{3}{14} + 9\dfrac{6}{7} =$

9

Picture It

When fractions have the same denominator, subtract them by subtracting the numerators only. The denominator stays the same. SUBTRACT the fractions and WRITE the difference.

HINT: Cross out the same number of boxes as the numerator of the second fraction to help you subtract.

Example:

$$\frac{6}{7} - \frac{2}{7} = \frac{4}{7}$$

1.

$$\frac{4}{5} - \frac{3}{5} = \underline{\quad}$$

2.

$$\frac{9}{10} - \frac{6}{10} = \underline{\quad}$$

3.

$$\frac{3}{6} - \frac{1}{6} = \underline{\quad}$$

4.

$$\frac{7}{12} - \frac{2}{12} = \underline{\quad}$$

5.

$$\frac{8}{8} - \frac{3}{8} = \underline{\quad}$$

6.

$$\frac{7}{9} - \frac{5}{9} = \underline{\quad}$$

Subtracting Fractions

Simple Differences

WRITE each difference as a fraction in its simplest form.

Examples: $\dfrac{11}{16} - \dfrac{3}{16} = \dfrac{8}{16} = \dfrac{1}{2}$ $\qquad$ $\dfrac{15}{7} - \dfrac{2}{7} = \dfrac{13}{7} = 1\dfrac{6}{7}$

$\dfrac{7}{8} - \dfrac{3}{8} =$

1

$\dfrac{11}{12} - \dfrac{2}{12} =$

2

$\dfrac{17}{21} - \dfrac{10}{21} =$

3

$\dfrac{17}{18} - \dfrac{15}{18} =$

4

$\dfrac{29}{24} - \dfrac{7}{24} =$

5

$\dfrac{24}{17} - \dfrac{7}{17} =$

6

$\dfrac{17}{13} - \dfrac{2}{13} =$

7

$\dfrac{42}{9} - \dfrac{14}{9} =$

8

$\dfrac{34}{25} - \dfrac{4}{25} =$

9

$\dfrac{27}{32} - \dfrac{3}{32} =$

10

Dueling Denominators

Find the lowest common denominator before subtracting.

Example: $\dfrac{7}{15} - \dfrac{3}{10} =$ $\dfrac{7 \times 2}{15 \times 2} = \dfrac{14}{30}$ $\dfrac{3 \times 3}{10 \times 3} = \dfrac{9}{30}$ $\dfrac{14}{30} - \dfrac{9}{30} = \dfrac{5}{30} = \dfrac{1}{6}$

REWRITE the fractions with their lowest common denominators. Then WRITE the difference as a fraction in its simplest form.

$\dfrac{1}{2} - \dfrac{2}{5} =$ ___ 1

$\dfrac{5}{6} - \dfrac{1}{4} =$ ___ 2

$\dfrac{7}{8} - \dfrac{3}{5} =$ ___ 3

$\dfrac{3}{4} - \dfrac{7}{12} =$ ___ 4

$\dfrac{1}{3} - \dfrac{2}{9} =$ ___ 5

$\dfrac{17}{24} - \dfrac{1}{4} =$ ___ 6

$\dfrac{5}{3} - \dfrac{1}{6} =$ ___ 7

$\dfrac{9}{5} - \dfrac{2}{3} =$ ___ 8

$\dfrac{15}{4} - \dfrac{3}{10} =$ ___ 9

Subtracting Fractions

Mixed Up

When subtracting mixed numbers, subtract the fractions, then the whole numbers.

$$6\frac{3}{4}$$
$$-\,3\frac{1}{2}$$
___
$$\frac{1}{4}$$

$$6\frac{3}{4}$$
$$-\,3\frac{2}{4}$$
___

$$6\frac{3}{4}$$
$$-\,3\frac{2}{4}$$
___
$$3\frac{1}{4}$$

If the smaller fraction is on top, then regrouping is necessary.

$$7\frac{1}{3}$$
$$-\,1\frac{1}{2}$$
___

$$7\frac{2}{6}$$
$$-\,1\frac{3}{6}$$
___

$$\cancel{7}^{6}\frac{8}{6}$$
$$-\,1\frac{3}{6}$$
___

$$1 = \frac{6}{6}$$

$$\frac{6}{6} + \frac{2}{6} = \frac{8}{6}$$

$$\cancel{7}^{6}\frac{8}{6}$$
$$-\,1\frac{3}{6}$$
___
$$5\frac{5}{6}$$

WRITE each difference as a fraction in its simplest form.

1.
$$4\frac{4}{7}$$
$$-\,2\frac{3}{7}$$
___

2.
$$9\frac{7}{9}$$
$$-\,2\frac{1}{9}$$
___

3.
$$6\frac{7}{12}$$
$$-\,3\frac{1}{12}$$
___

4.
$$7\frac{9}{10}$$
$$-\,6\frac{4}{5}$$
___

5.
$$10\frac{2}{3}$$
$$-\,1\frac{5}{9}$$
___

6.
$$8\frac{5}{7}$$
$$-\,4\frac{1}{2}$$
___

7.
$$5\frac{1}{4}$$
$$-\,2\frac{5}{8}$$
___

8.
$$2\frac{2}{5}$$
$$-\,1\frac{11}{15}$$
___

9.
$$11\frac{5}{6}$$
$$-\,5\frac{8}{9}$$
___

Picture It

When a number is multiplied by a fraction that is less than one, the product will be a smaller number.

Multiplying 8 by $\frac{1}{4}$ is like looking for $\frac{1}{4}$ of 8.

$$8 \times \frac{1}{4} = 2$$

Multiplying $\frac{1}{3}$ by $\frac{1}{2}$ is like looking for $\frac{1}{2}$ of $\frac{1}{3}$.

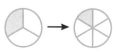

$$\frac{1}{3} \times \frac{1}{2} = \frac{1}{6}$$

Use the pictures to help you answer the problems. WRITE each product.

1.

$$7 \times \frac{1}{7} =$$

2.

$$10 \times \frac{1}{2} =$$

3.

$$9 \times \frac{1}{3} =$$

4.

$$1 \times \frac{1}{5} = \underline{\quad}$$

5.

$$\frac{1}{2} \times \frac{1}{4} = \underline{\quad}$$

6.

$$\frac{2}{3} \times \frac{1}{3} = \underline{\quad}$$

Multiplying Fractions

Straight Across

To multiply fractions, multiply the numerators, multiply the denominators, and then write the product in its simplest form.

Example: $\dfrac{4}{5} \times \dfrac{1}{2} = \dfrac{4 \times 1}{5 \times 2} = \dfrac{4}{10} = \dfrac{2}{5}$

WRITE each product as a fraction in its simplest form.

$\dfrac{1}{5} \times \dfrac{1}{3} = $ _____

1

$\dfrac{2}{5} \times \dfrac{1}{4} = $ _____

2

$\dfrac{6}{7} \times \dfrac{1}{3} = $ _____

3

$\dfrac{4}{9} \times \dfrac{5}{6} = $ _____

4

$\dfrac{3}{8} \times \dfrac{2}{3} = $ _____

5

$\dfrac{1}{12} \times \dfrac{3}{5} = $ _____

6

$\dfrac{3}{4} \times \dfrac{3}{7} = $ _____

7

$\dfrac{5}{7} \times \dfrac{1}{10} = $ _____

8

$\dfrac{3}{8} \times \dfrac{5}{10} = $ _____

9

Simply Simplify

You can make multiplication easier by first simplifying the fractions.

$$\frac{3}{7} \times \frac{1}{9} = \frac{3 \times 1}{7 \times 9} = \frac{3}{63}$$

$$\frac{3 \div 3}{63 \div 3} = \frac{1}{21}$$

You know how to simplify after multiplying.

$$\frac{3}{7} \times \frac{1}{9} =$$

To simplify before multiplying, look for common factors in the numerator of one fraction and the denominator of the other. The numerator 3 is a factor of 3 and 9.

$$\overset{1}{\cancel{3}}{} \times \frac{1}{\underset{3}{\cancel{9}}} = \frac{1}{21}$$

$3 \div 3 = 1$
Cross out 3 and write 1.
$9 \div 3 = 3$
Cross out 9 and write 3.
Multiply the simplified fractions to find the product.

First, SIMPLIFY the fractions. Then WRITE the product.

$$\frac{2}{5} \times \frac{3}{4} = \underline{\quad\quad}$$
1

$$\frac{3}{7} \times \frac{5}{12} = \underline{\quad\quad}$$
2

$$\frac{5}{6} \times \frac{6}{11} = \underline{\quad\quad}$$
3

$$\frac{5}{8} \times \frac{9}{20} = \underline{\quad\quad}$$
4

$$\frac{9}{4} \times \frac{7}{18} = \underline{\quad\quad}$$
5

$$\frac{11}{32} \times \frac{8}{9} = \underline{\quad\quad}$$
6

$$\frac{4}{7} \times \frac{7}{24} = \underline{\quad\quad}$$
7

$$\frac{9}{10} \times \frac{5}{6} = \underline{\quad\quad}$$
8

$$\frac{6}{15} \times \frac{5}{9} = \underline{\quad\quad}$$
9

Mixed Up

To multiply, change the mixed numbers to improper fractions. Simplify, and then multiply.

Examples:

$$3\frac{1}{5} \times 2\frac{1}{4} =$$

$$3\frac{1}{5} \times 2\frac{1}{4} = \frac{16}{5} \times \frac{9}{4} = \frac{\overset{4}{\cancel{16}}}{5} \times \frac{9}{\underset{1}{\cancel{4}}} = \frac{36}{5} = 7\frac{1}{5}$$

$$4 \times 5\frac{1}{6} = \frac{4}{1} \times \frac{31}{6} = \frac{\overset{2}{\cancel{4}}}{1} \times \frac{31}{\underset{3}{\cancel{6}}} = \frac{62}{3} = 20\frac{2}{3}$$

WRITE the product as a fraction in its simplest form.

$$1\frac{1}{6} \times 2\frac{2}{3} = \boxed{}$$

1

$$3\frac{3}{4} \times 4\frac{1}{5} = \boxed{}$$

2

$$3\frac{3}{5} \times 1\frac{2}{3} = \boxed{}$$

3

$$6\frac{2}{7} \times 1\frac{1}{6} = \boxed{}$$

4

$$2\frac{1}{2} \times 3\frac{1}{5} = \boxed{}$$

5

$$4\frac{2}{5} \times 3\frac{3}{4} = \boxed{}$$

6

$$3 \times 7\frac{2}{9} = \boxed{}$$

7

$$5 \times 1\frac{1}{20} = \boxed{}$$

8

$$10 \times 6\frac{4}{5} = \boxed{}$$

9

Radical Reciprocals

A **reciprocal** of a fraction is its inverse, which means that the numbers in the numerator and the denominator switch places.

HINT: To find the reciprocal of a fraction, flip it upside down.

Examples: The reciprocal of $\frac{3}{4}$ is $\frac{4}{3}$.   The reciprocal of 5 is $\frac{1}{5}$.

WRITE each reciprocal.

$\frac{5}{6}$ _____

1

$\frac{7}{2}$ _____

2

$\frac{1}{3}$ _____

3

$\frac{9}{10}$ _____

4

$\frac{12}{5}$ _____

5

$\frac{1}{11}$ _____

6

$\frac{8}{5}$ _____

7

8 _____

8

$\frac{4}{13}$ _____

9

$\frac{32}{23}$ _____

10

$\frac{55}{67}$ _____

11

$\frac{99}{100}$ _____

12

The One and Only

The product of a fraction and its reciprocal is always 1.

$$\frac{2}{5} \times \frac{5}{2} = \frac{10}{10} = 1 \qquad\qquad \frac{3}{7} \times \frac{7}{3} = \frac{\overset{1}{\cancel{3}}}{\underset{1}{\cancel{7}}} \times \frac{\overset{1}{\cancel{7}}}{\underset{1}{\cancel{3}}} = \frac{1}{1} = 1$$

WRITE each missing factor or product.

$$\frac{6}{7} \times \frac{7}{6} = \boxed{}$$

1

$$\frac{2}{11} \times \frac{11}{2} = \boxed{}$$

2

$$3\frac{1}{4} \times \frac{4}{13} = \boxed{}$$

3

$$\frac{4}{3} \times \boxed{} = 1$$

4

$$\frac{8}{9} \times \boxed{} = 1$$

5

$$3 \times \boxed{} = 1$$

6

$$\boxed{} \times \frac{17}{6} = 1$$

7

$$\boxed{} \times \frac{78}{103} = 1$$

8

$$\boxed{} \times 5\frac{5}{6} = 1$$

9

Picture It

When a number is divided by a fraction that is less than one, the product will be a bigger number.

Dividing 3 by $\frac{1}{8}$ is like looking for the number of eighths in 3.

$\frac{1}{8}$ is found in 3 a total of 24 times. $3 \div \frac{1}{8} = 24$.

Dividing $\frac{1}{2}$ by $\frac{1}{4}$ is like looking for the number of fourths in one half.

$\frac{1}{4}$ is found in $\frac{1}{2}$ a total of 2 times. $\frac{1}{2} \div \frac{1}{4} = 2$

Use the pictures to help you answer the problems. WRITE each quotient.

1.

$4 \div \frac{1}{3} =$

2.

$5 \div \frac{1}{2} =$

3.
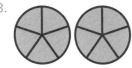

$2 \div \frac{2}{5} =$

4.

$\frac{3}{4} \div \frac{1}{4} =$

5.

$\frac{1}{2} \div \frac{1}{8} =$

6.

$\frac{5}{6} \div \frac{5}{12} =$

Dividing Fractions

Flip and Multiply

To divide fractions, multiply by the reciprocal of the divisor.

$$\frac{6}{7} \div \frac{2}{3} = \frac{6}{7} \times \frac{3}{2} = \frac{\overset{3}{\cancel{6}}}{7} \times \frac{3}{\underset{1}{\cancel{2}}} = \frac{9}{7} = 1\frac{2}{7}$$

WRITE each quotient as a fraction in its simplest form.

$\frac{3}{4} \div \frac{2}{5} =$

1

$\frac{1}{6} \div \frac{2}{3} =$

2

$\frac{7}{15} \div \frac{4}{5} =$

3

$\frac{7}{8} \div 7 =$

4

$\frac{4}{9} \div \frac{1}{15} =$

5

$\frac{5}{14} \div \frac{5}{7} =$

6

$\frac{9}{32} \div \frac{3}{8} =$

7

$\frac{7}{16} \div \frac{3}{40} =$

8

$\frac{18}{19} \div \frac{27}{38} =$

9

Mixed Up

To divide, change the mixed numbers to improper fractions.

Examples: $2\frac{4}{7} \div 1\frac{1}{5} =$ $2\frac{4}{7} \div 1\frac{1}{5} = \frac{18}{7} \div \frac{6}{5} = \frac{18}{7} \times \frac{5}{6} = \frac{\overset{3}{\cancel{18}}}{7} \times \frac{5}{\underset{1}{\cancel{6}}} = \frac{15}{7} = 2\frac{1}{7}$

WRITE each quotient as a fraction in its simplest form.

$3\frac{3}{4} \div 2\frac{1}{2} =$ ⬜
1

$1\frac{1}{5} \div 5\frac{2}{5} =$ ⬜
2

$2\frac{5}{9} \div 2\frac{1}{3} =$ ⬜
3

$1\frac{1}{2} \div 3\frac{3}{8} =$ ⬜
4

$4\frac{1}{2} \div 4\frac{1}{4} =$ ⬜
5

$5\frac{5}{6} \div 10 =$ ⬜
6

$9 \div 3\frac{3}{5} =$ ⬜
7

$8\frac{4}{9} \div 4 =$ ⬜
8

$2\frac{7}{9} \div 15 =$ ⬜
9

Fraction Action

WRITE the answers.

1. How many $\frac{1}{2}$ miles are in 37 miles? _____

2. How many $\frac{1}{4}$ hours are in 24 hours? _____

3. How many $\frac{1}{12}$ inches are in 10 inches? _____

4. How many $\frac{1}{4}$ pounds are in 90 pounds? _____

5. How many $\frac{1}{2}$ dollars are in 52 dollars? _____

6. How many $\frac{1}{10}$ feet are in 18 feet? _____

7. How many $\frac{1}{3}$ yards are in 123 yards? _____

8. How many $\frac{1}{6}$ dozen are in 15 dozen? _____

Unit Rewind

WRITE each sum or difference as a fraction in its simplest form.

$\dfrac{1}{6} + \dfrac{5}{6} =$

1

$\dfrac{4}{9} + \dfrac{7}{9} =$

2

$\dfrac{4}{15} + \dfrac{2}{5} =$

3

$\dfrac{8}{21} + \dfrac{6}{7} =$

4

$5\dfrac{1}{3} + 2\dfrac{5}{9} =$

5

$3\dfrac{1}{2} + 8\dfrac{13}{16} =$

6

7. $\dfrac{7}{13}$
$-\dfrac{4}{13}$

8. $\dfrac{5}{8}$
$-\dfrac{1}{8}$

9. $\dfrac{11}{16}$
$-\dfrac{5}{8}$

10. $\dfrac{2}{3}$
$-\dfrac{1}{5}$

11. $8\dfrac{7}{9}$
$-4\dfrac{2}{3}$

12. $12\dfrac{2}{7}$
$-5\dfrac{4}{5}$

Unit Rewind

WRITE each product or quotient as a fraction in its simplest form.

$\dfrac{1}{8} \times \dfrac{2}{3} =$

1

$\dfrac{2}{9} \times \dfrac{1}{12} =$

2

$\dfrac{3}{5} \times \dfrac{15}{24} =$

3

$\dfrac{5}{19} \times \dfrac{19}{5} =$

4

$\dfrac{6}{7} \times 1\dfrac{1}{6} =$

5

$2\dfrac{4}{5} \times 6\dfrac{1}{7} =$

6

$\dfrac{2}{5} \div \dfrac{7}{10} =$

7

$\dfrac{9}{10} \div \dfrac{3}{4} =$

8

$\dfrac{3}{7} \div \dfrac{1}{4} =$

9

$5\dfrac{1}{9} \div 7\dfrac{2}{3} =$

10

$3 \div \dfrac{1}{6} =$

11

$\dfrac{4}{5} \div 24 =$

12

Shoes in a Foot

MEASURE the length of each shoe in inches and answer the questions. WRITE the answers as a fraction or mixed number.

HINT: 1 foot (ft) = 12 inches (in.)   1 yard (yd) = 3 ft = 36 in.

_____ in.

1

_____ in.

2

How many of each kind of shoe would fit end to end in one foot?

_____ red shoes   _____ sneakers

3   4

How many of each kind of shoe would fit end to end in one yard?

_____ red shoes   _____ sneakers

5   6

Fitting In

MEASURE the width of the book, DVD, and CD in centimeters and ANSWER the questions. WRITE the answers as decimals.

HINT: 1 meter (m) = 100 centimeters (cm)

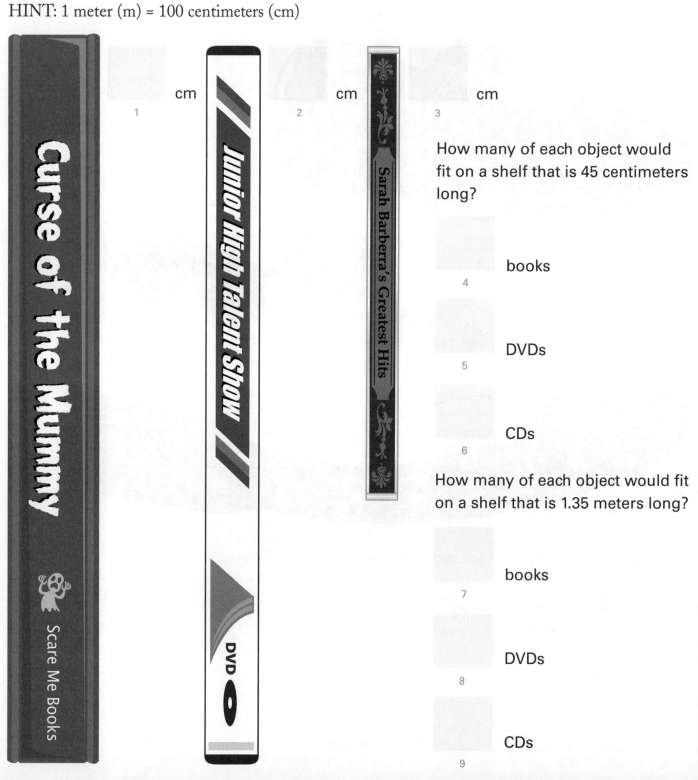

_____ cm
1

_____ cm
2

_____ cm
3

How many of each object would fit on a shelf that is 45 centimeters long?

_____ books
4

_____ DVDs
5

_____ CDs
6

How many of each object would fit on a shelf that is 1.35 meters long?

_____ books
7

_____ DVDs
8

_____ CDs
9

Around We Go

Perimeter is the distance around a two-dimensional shape. To find the perimeter, add the lengths of all of the sides. For shapes with sides that are the same length, multiply the length of one side by the number of sides.

4 in.

7 in.

7 + 4 + 7 + 4 = 22
The perimeter of this rectangle is 22 in.

6 cm

6 × 3 = 18
The perimeter of this triangle is 18 cm.

WRITE the perimeter of each shape.

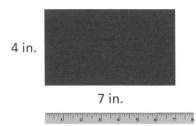

2 cm

7 cm

_____ cm

1

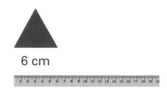

_____ cm

2

10 cm

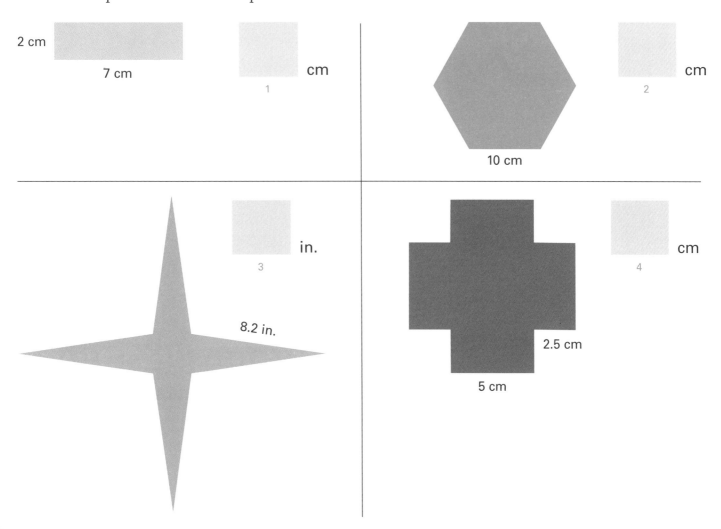

_____ in.

3

8.2 in.

_____ cm

4

2.5 cm

5 cm

Perimeter

Around the Yard

WRITE the perimeter of the yard and each object in it.

1. Yard: _____ yd

2. Table: _____ in.

3. Garden: _____ ft

4. Sandbox: _____ ft

Angle Untangle

An **angle** is formed when two lines meet, and it is measured in degrees using a protractor. There are three different types of angles: right, acute, and obtuse.

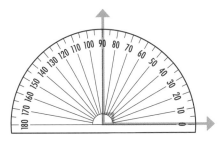

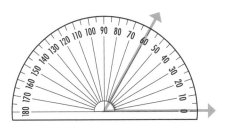

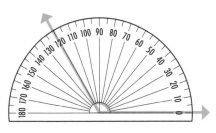

A **right** angle is an angle measuring exactly 90°, indicated by the ⌐ symbol in the corner.

An **acute** angle is any angle measuring less than 90°.

An **obtuse** angle is any angle measuring more than 90°.

WRITE *right*, *acute*, or *obtuse* for each angle.

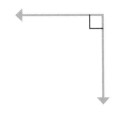

1. _____

2. _____

3. _____

4. _____

5. _____

6. _____

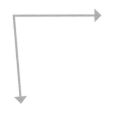

7. _____

8. _____

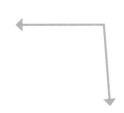

9. _____

Circle the Same

CIRCLE all of the angles that are in the correct column.

Right	Acute	Obtuse

Hidden Angles

Two sides of a shape meet to form an angle.

Example:

A square has four right angles.

WRITE the number of right, acute, and obtuse angles in each shape.

	Right Angles	Acute Angles	Obtuse Angles

Measure Up

MEASURE each angle using a protractor. WRITE the approximate measurement.

HINT: If you don't have a protractor, cut out the one in the example.

Example:

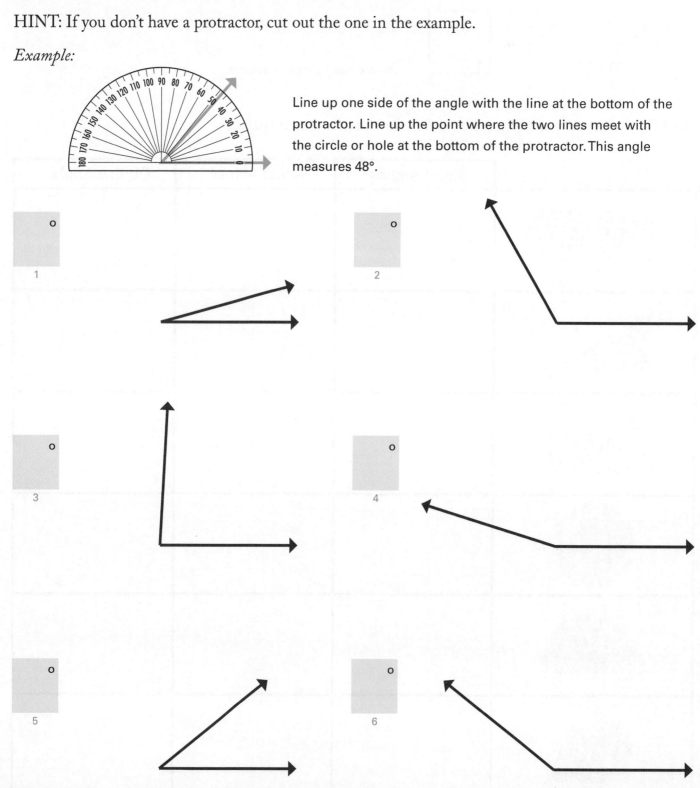

Line up one side of the angle with the line at the bottom of the protractor. Line up the point where the two lines meet with the circle or hole at the bottom of the protractor. This angle measures 48°.

1 °

2 °

3 °

4 °

5 °

6 °

Circle the Same

A **point** marks a place in space, represented by a dot.

A **line** is a straight path that has no end in either direction.

A **line segment** is the part of a line between two points, called **endpoints**.

A **ray** is a line that begins at an endpoint and has no end in the other direction.

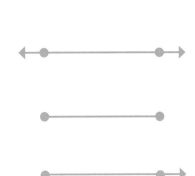

CIRCLE the name in each row that matches the picture.

1. line segment   point   ray

2. line   line segment   point

3. ray   point   line

4. line   line segment   ray

5. ray   line   endpoint

Points, Lines & Rays

What's My Name?

Letters are used to name points, lines, and rays.

A point is named by a single letter: *A*

Two points on a line are used to name the line: $\overleftrightarrow{AB}$ or $\overleftrightarrow{BA}$

The endpoints are used to name a line segment: $\overline{AB}$ or $\overline{BA}$

The endpoint and another point on the line name a ray: $\overrightarrow{AB}$
The endpoint is listed first.

WRITE the name of each point, line, or ray.

1. _____

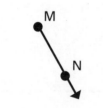

4. _____

7. _____

Q   R
●————————●—→

2. _____

8. _____

F
●

3. _____

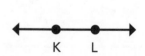

6. _____

9. _____

C————D

5. _____

Match Up

DRAW a line to connect each name to the correct line, point, or ray.

A   A •———————•B→

$\overline{AB}$ A•

$\overrightarrow{BA}$ A•————————•B

B   ←•B————•A→

$\overrightarrow{AB}$ ←•A————•B

$\overleftrightarrow{BA}$ B•

Circle the Same

Intersecting lines are lines that cross one another.

Perpendicular lines intersect to form right angles.

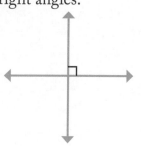

Parallel lines never intersect and are always the same distance apart.

CIRCLE all of the lines that are in the correct column.

Intersecting	Perpendicular	Parallel

Fine Lines

FIND each pair of lines in the picture. Then WRITE *parallel*, *perpendicular*, or *intersecting* to describe the lines.

HINT: Some will have more than one correct answer.

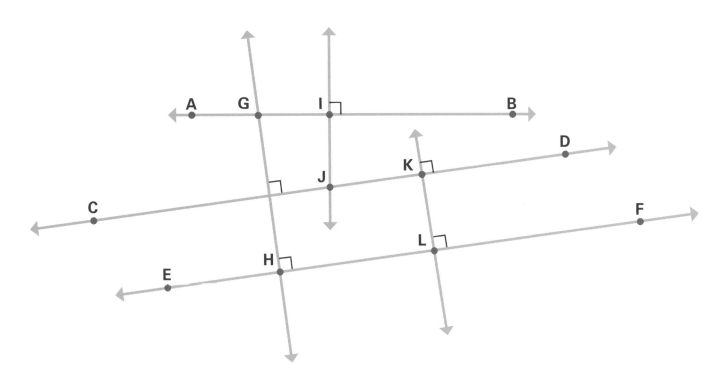

1. $\overleftrightarrow{CD}$ and $\overleftrightarrow{EF}$ _____

2. $\overleftrightarrow{AB}$ and $\overleftrightarrow{GH}$ _____

3. $\overleftrightarrow{CD}$ and $\overleftrightarrow{KL}$ _____

4. $\overleftrightarrow{GH}$ and $\overleftrightarrow{KL}$ _____

5. $\overleftrightarrow{KL}$ and $\overleftrightarrow{EF}$ _____

6. $\overleftrightarrow{AB}$ and $\overleftrightarrow{IJ}$ _____

7. $\overleftrightarrow{AB}$ and $\overleftrightarrow{CD}$ _____

Line Drawing

DRAW a picture to match each description.

1. $\overline{AB}$

2. $\overleftrightarrow{CD}$

3. $\overrightarrow{EF}$

4. $\overline{GH}$ parallel to $\overline{IJ}$

5. $\overleftrightarrow{KL}$ intersecting $\overleftrightarrow{MN}$

6. $\overleftrightarrow{OP}$ perpendicular $\overleftrightarrow{QR}$

Taking Shape

A **polygon** is a closed plane shape that has three or more sides. Polygons are named according to their number of sides.

 A **triangle** has three sides.

 A **heptagon** has seven sides.

 A **quadrilateral** has four sides.

 An **octagon** has eight sides.

 A **pentagon** has five sides.

 A **nonagon** has nine sides.

 A **hexagon** has six sides.

 A **decagon** has ten sides.

WRITE the name of each polygon.

1. _____

2. _____

3. _____

4. _____

5. _____

6. _____

7. _____

8. _____

Taking Shape

A **quadrilateral** is a polygon with four sides, and there are several specific types of quadrilaterals.

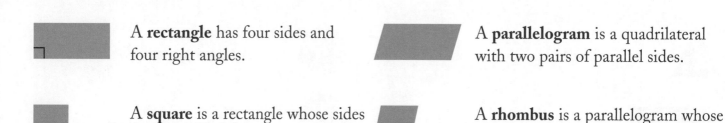

A **rectangle** has four sides and four right angles.

A **parallelogram** is a quadrilateral with two pairs of parallel sides.

A **square** is a rectangle whose sides are all of equal length.

A **rhombus** is a parallelogram whose sides are all of equal length.

A **trapezoid** is a quadrilateral with only one pair of parallel sides.

WRITE the name of each quadrilateral.

HINT: Some will have more than one correct answer.

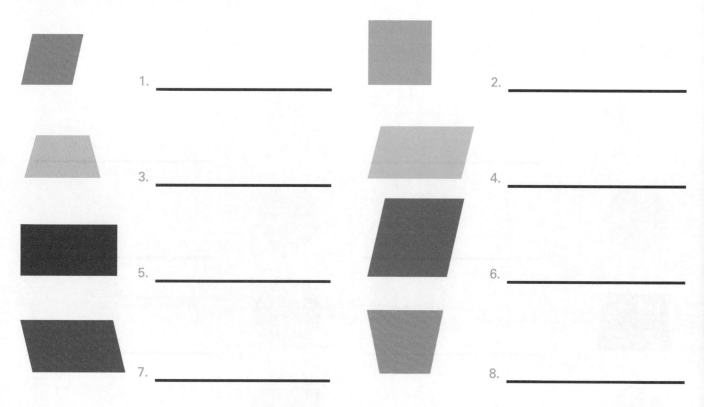

1. _____

2. _____

3. _____

4. _____

5. _____

6. _____

7. _____

8. _____

Shape Up

A **vertex** is the point where two sides meet.

Example: vertex ⟶ ○

A triangle has three vertices.

WRITE the name of each shape and the number of its sides, vertices, and pairs of vertical lines.

	Shape Name	Number of Sides	Number of Vertices	Pairs of Parallel Lines

Circle the Same

A shape is **congruent** to another if it is exactly the same shape and size.

These two shapes are congruent. Even though one is turned, it is still the same size and shape as the other.

These two shapes are not congruent. The second is not exactly the same size and shape as the first.

CIRCLE the shape that is congruent to the first shape.

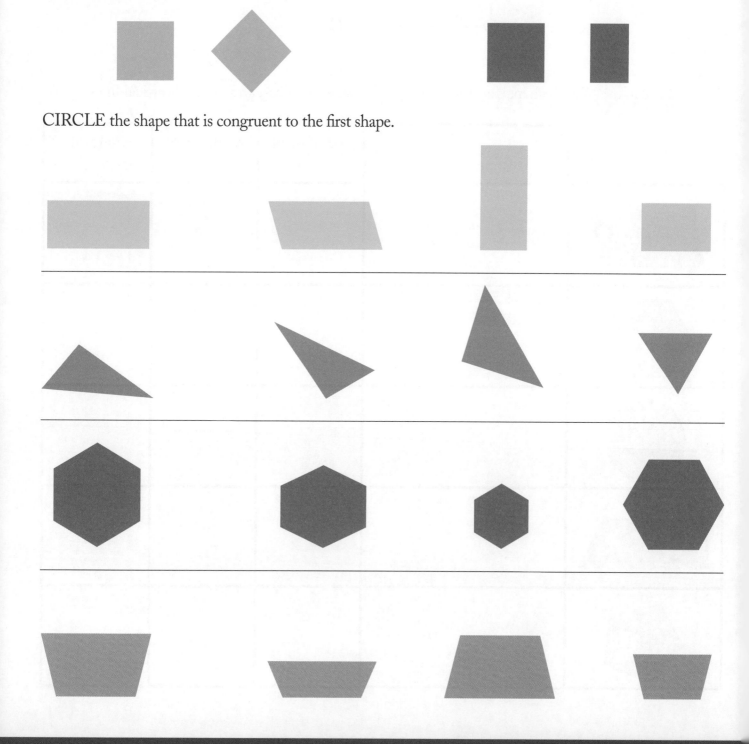

Rectangle Range

Area is the size of the surface of a shape, and it is measured in square units. Find the area of a rectangle by multiplying the length by the width.

Example: 2 in.   2 inches × 3 inches = 6 square inches (sq in.)

3 in.

WRITE the area of each rectangle.

7 cm

10 cm

1. _____ sq cm

5 in.

2. _____ sq in.

23 cm

28 cm

15 in.

32 in.

3. _____ sq cm

4. _____ sq in.

$3\frac{3}{4}$ ft

8 ft

4.8 m

5. _____ sq ft

6. _____ sq m

Tricky Triangles

Find the area of a triangle by multiplying $\frac{1}{2}$ times the base of the triangle times the height of the triangle.

Examples:

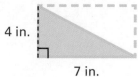

$$\frac{1}{2} \times 7 \times 4 = \frac{28}{2} = 14$$

Area = 14 sq in.

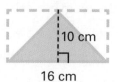

$$\frac{1}{2} \times 16 \times 10 = \frac{160}{2} = 80$$

Area = 80 sq cm

WRITE the area of each triangle.

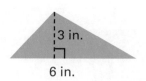

1. _____ sq in.

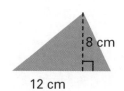

2. _____ sq cm

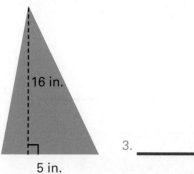

3. _____ sq in.

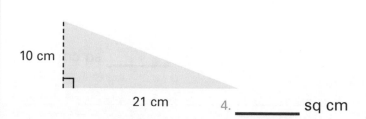

4. _____ sq cm

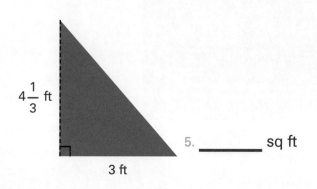

5. _____ sq ft

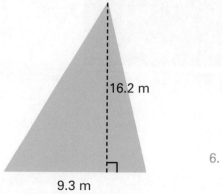

6. _____ sq m

Parallelogram Patch

Find the area of a parallelogram by multiplying the base times the height.

Example:

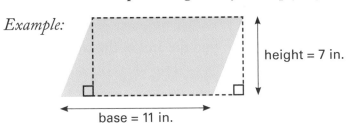

height = 7 in.

base = 11 in.

Area = 11 × 7 = 77 sq in.

The height of a parallelogram is the distance between parallel sides as measured by a perpendicular line.

WRITE the area of each parallelogram.

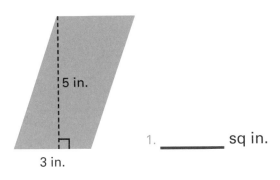

5 in.

3 in.

1. _____ sq in.

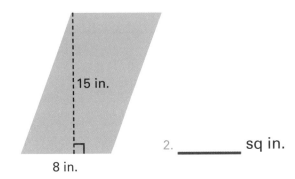

15 in.

8 in.

2. _____ sq in.

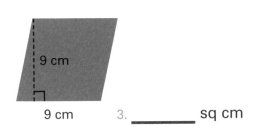

9 cm

9 cm

3. _____ sq cm

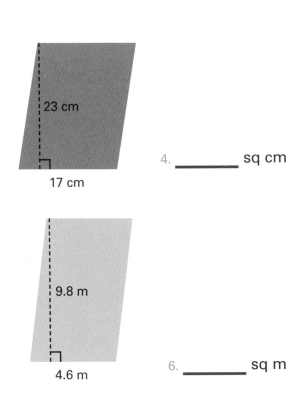

23 cm

17 cm

4. _____ sq cm

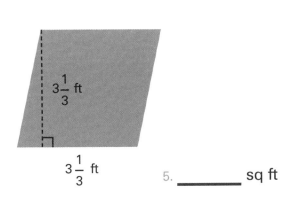

$3\frac{1}{3}$ ft

$3\frac{1}{3}$ ft

5. _____ sq ft

9.8 m

4.6 m

6. _____ sq m

Put It Together

LOOK for the rectangles, triangles, and parallelograms in the shapes. Use the measurements provided, and WRITE the area of each shape.

HINT: Find the area of the individual shapes, then add them together to find the area of the larger shape.

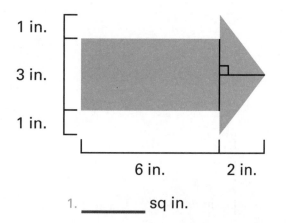

1. _____ sq in.

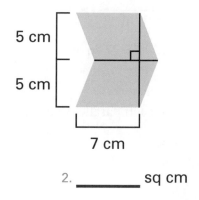

2. _____ sq cm

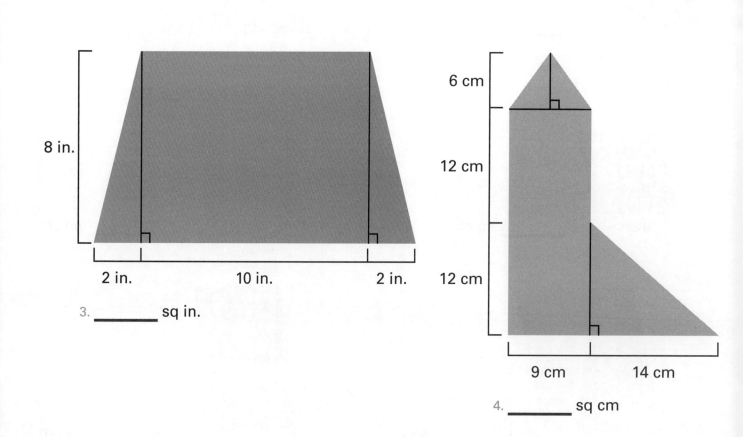

3. _____ sq in.

4. _____ sq cm

Taking Shape

Solid shapes are three-dimensional shapes.

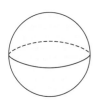
sphere

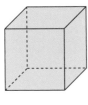
cube

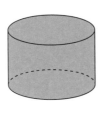
cylinder

cone

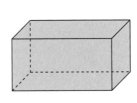
rectangular prism

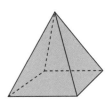
square pyramid

WRITE the name of each solid shape.

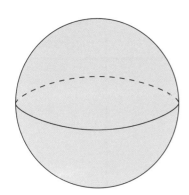

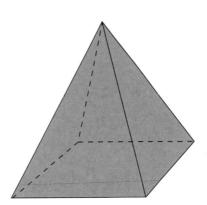

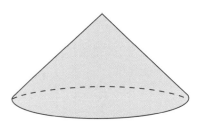

1. _____ 2. _____ 3. _____

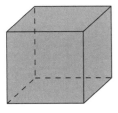

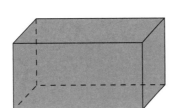

4. _____ 5. _____ 6. _____

Shape Up

In a three-dimensional shape, a **vertex** is where three or more edges meet. An **edge** is where two sides meet. A **face** is the shape formed by the edges.

Example:

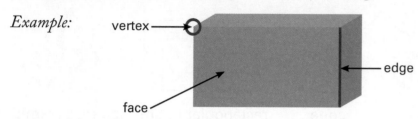

WRITE the name of each shape and the number of its vertices, edges, and faces.

	Shape Name	Number of Vertices	Number of Edges	Number of Faces

Squared Away

Volume is the measure of cubic units that fit inside a space.

Example:

1 cubic unit

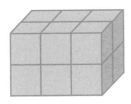

12 cubic units

WRITE the volume of each shape in cubic units.

1. _____ cubic units

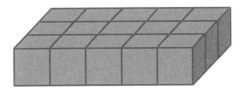

2. _____ cubic units

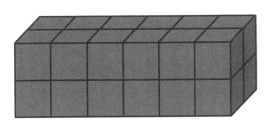

3. _____ cubic units

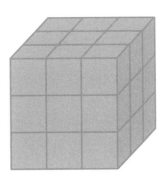

4. _____ cubic units

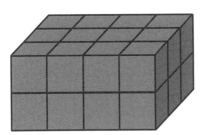

5. _____ cubic units

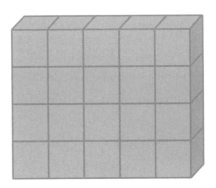

6. _____ cubic units

Speaking Volumes

Find the volume of a rectangular prism by multiplying the length times the width times the height.

Example:

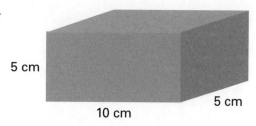

5 cm
10 cm
5 cm

Volume = 10 × 5 × 5

Volume = 250 cubic centimeters = 250 cm³

WRITE the volume of each shape in cubic units.

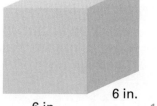

6 in.
6 in.
6 in.

1. _____ in.³

8 cm
10 cm
2 cm

2. _____ cm³

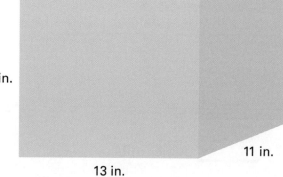

13 in.
13 in.
11 in.

3. _____ in.³

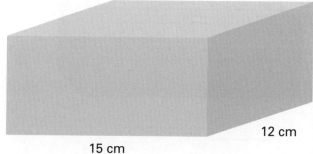

25 cm
15 cm
12 cm

4. _____ cm³

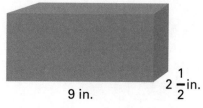

4 in.
9 in.
2 ½ in.

5. _____ in.³

5.2 cm
4.6 cm
7 cm

6. _____ cm³

Maximum Volume

WRITE the volume of each object. Then WRITE the answers to the questions.

5 in.

11 in.

7 in.

1. _____ in.³

10 in.

13 in.

13 in.

2. _____ in.³

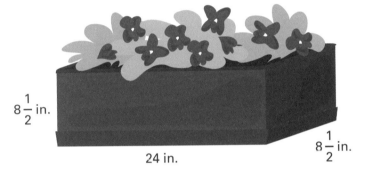

$8\frac{1}{2}$ in.

24 in.

$8\frac{1}{2}$ in.

3. _____ in.³

13 in.

3 in.

$9\frac{1}{2}$ in.

4. _____ in.³

$12\frac{1}{2}$ in.

4 in.

$17\frac{1}{2}$ in.

5. _____ in.³

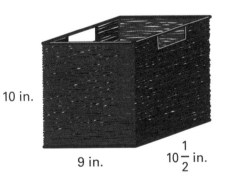

10 in.

9 in.

$10\frac{1}{2}$ in.

6. _____ in.³

7. Which object has the greatest volume? _____

8. Which object has the least volume? _____

Volume

Missing Pieces

WRITE the volume of each shape.

HINT: Find the volume as though the shape were a complete rectangular prism, and then subtract the volume of the missing piece.

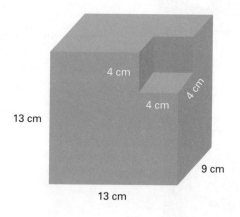

13 cm
4 cm
4 cm
4 cm
9 cm
13 cm

1. _____ cm³

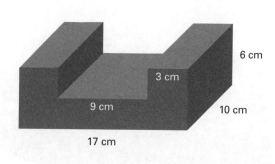

6 cm
3 cm
9 cm
10 cm
17 cm

2. _____ cm³

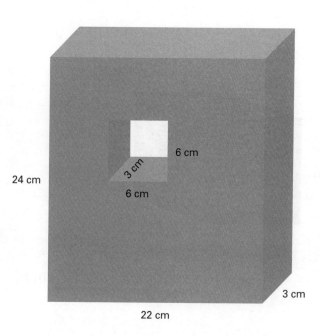

24 cm
6 cm
3 cm
6 cm
3 cm
22 cm

3. _____ cm³

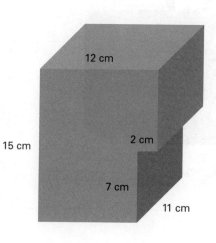

12 cm
15 cm
2 cm
7 cm
11 cm

4. _____ cm³

Unit Rewind

WRITE the word that matches each picture.

ray	cylinder	heptagon	parallel lines
pentagon	obtuse angle	square pyramid	perpendicular lines
sphere	point	line segment	acute angle

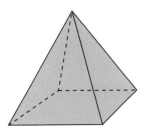

1. _____

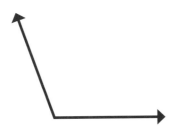

2. _____

3. _____

4. _____

5. _____

6. _____

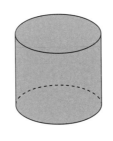

7. _____

8. _____

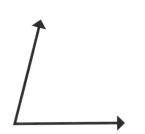

9. _____

10. _____

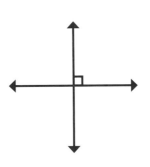

11. _____

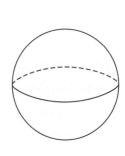

12. _____

Unit Rewind

WRITE the approximate measurement of each angle.

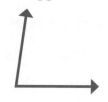

1. _____

2. _____

3. _____

WRITE the perimeter and area of each shape.

4.

5 in.

8 in.

5.

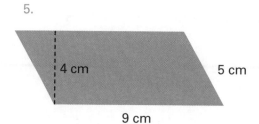

4 cm   5 cm

9 cm

6.

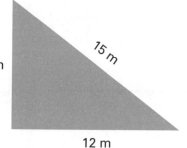

9 m   15 m

12 m

Perimeter _____ in.

Area _____ sq in.

Perimeter _____ cm

Area _____ sq cm

Perimeter _____ sq m

Area _____ sq m

WRITE the volume of each rectangular prism.

3 in.

5 in.   9 in.

4.7 cm

6.3 cm   12 cm

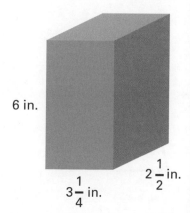

6 in.

$3\frac{1}{4}$ in. $2\frac{1}{2}$ in.

7. _____ in.³

8. _____ cm³

9. _____ in.³

Answers

Page 3
1. 8, 16, 32
2. 6, 12, 24
3. 9, 27, 81
4. 6, 18, 54
5. 5, 25, 125

Page 4
1. 8; 80; 800; 8,000; 80,000; 800,000
2. 42; 420; 4,200; 42,000; 420,000; 4,200,000
3. 6; 60; 600; 6,000; 60,000; 600,000
4. 36; 360; 3,600; 36,000; 360,000; 3,600,000

Page 5
1. 168
2. 455
3. 392

Page 6
1. 135
2. 312
3. 91
4. 296
5. 544
6. 170
7. 1,589
8. 1,178
9. 3,220
10. 2,848
11. 6,965
12. 1,788
13. 6,651
14. 1,518
15. 1,376
16. 3,716
17. 3,420
18. 7,785

Page 7
1. 540
2. 2,112
3. 630
4. 1,568
5. 1,748
6. 1,116
7. 3,384
8. 4,611
9. 1,300
10. 1,716
11. 3,944
12. 306
13. 4,888
14. 2,754
15. 1,125
16. 4,355
17. 5,841
18. 6,552

Page 8
1. 19,825
2. 44,454
3. 54,056
4. 18,705
5. 41,366
6. 49,379
7. 25,970
8. 6,698
9. 73,892
10. 11,165
11. 27,335
12. 55,112
13. 33,024
14. 73,242
15. 13,554
16. 25,002
17. 22,737
18. 57,350

Page 9
1. 129,864
2. 165,105
3. 324,918
4. 434,408
5. 343,542
6. 238,304
7. 168,350
8. 197,802
9. 214,896
10. 303,450
11. 1,394,672
12. 2,564,800
13. 739,383
14. 1,667,624
15. 4,019,089

Page 10
1. 248
2. 308
3. 806
4. 960
5. 1,240
6. 1,350
7. 1,460
8. 5,475
9. 8,760
10. 10,585
11. 13,505
12. 18,250

Page 11
1.
```
    296      300
  ×  24    ×  20
  -----    -----
  7,104    6,000
```
2.
```
    814      800
  ×  96    × 100
  ------   ------
 78,144   80,000
```
3.
```
    571      600
  × 935    × 900
 -------  -------
 533,885  540,000
```

Page 11 (continued)
4.
```
    707      700
  × 682    × 700
 -------  -------
 482,174  490,000
```
5.
```
   4,338    4,000
  ×  472   ×  500
 --------  --------
 2,047,536 2,000,000
```
6.
```
   9,566    10,000
  ×  343   ×   300
 --------  ---------
 3,281,138 3,000,000
```

Page 12

Page 13

Page 14
14: 1, 2, 7, 14
49: 1, 7, 49
Common factors: 1, 7
Greatest common factor: 7

20: 1, 2, 4, 5, 10, 20
32: 1, 2, 4, 8, 16, 32
Common factors: 1, 2, 4
Greatest common factor: 4

24: 1, 2, 3, 4, 6, 8, 12, 24
60: 1, 2, 3, 4, 5, 6, 10, 12, 15, 20, 30, 60
Common factors: 1, 2, 3, 4, 6, 12
Greatest common factor: 12

Page 15
1. 200; 2,000; 20,000
2. 108; 648; 3,888
3. 144; 1,728; 20,736
4. 900; 13,500; 202,500

Page 16
1.
```
    336      300
  × 189    × 200
 -------  -------
 63,504   60,000
```
2.
```
    623      600
  × 798    × 800
 -------  -------
 497,154  480,000
```
3.
```
   5,890    6,000
  ×  263   ×  300
 --------  ---------
 1,549,070 1,800,000
```

Page 16 (continued)
4.
```
   4,255    4,000
  ×  677   ×  700
 --------  ---------
 2,880,635 2,800,000
```

18: 1, 2, 3, 6, 9, 18
45: 1, 3, 5, 9, 15, 45
Common factors: 1, 3, 9
Greatest common factor: 9

Page 17
1. 2, 4, 8
2. 7, 14, 28
3. 1, 3, 9
4. 5, 15, 45
5. 5, 25, 125

Page 18
1. 4; 40; 40; 400; 400; 4,000
2. 3; 30; 30; 300; 300; 3,000
3. 2; 20; 20; 200; 200; 2,000
4. 9; 90; 90; 900; 900; 9,000

Page 19
1. 35
2. 59
3. 97
4. 19
5. 560
6. 919
7. 381
8. 754
9. 8,071
10. 7,343
11. 1,648
12. 4,592

Page 20
1. 81 r1
2. 78 r2
3. 58 r1
4. 94 r4
5. 537 r5
6. 343 r3
7. 801 r6
8. 359 r1
9. 9,796 r4
10. 6,415 r3
11. 8,774 r1
12. 1,628 r7

Page 21
1. 44
2. 17
3. 22
4. 39
5. 15 r2
6. 71 r1
7. 21 r8
8. 26 r22
9. 34 r5
10. 14 r4
11. 27 r26
12. 13 r14

Page 22
1. 177
2. 486
3. 113
4. 212
5. 226 r2
6. 304 r5
7. 184 r8
8. 425 r4
9. 326 r3
10. 135 r6
11. 194 r12
12. 367 r11

Page 23
1. 1,281
2. 1,687
3. 2,316
4. 1,263
5. 3,462 r2
6. 1,598 r8
7. 1,029 r23
8. 852 r10
9. 2,398 r7
10. 1,404 r20
11. 1,184 r35
12. 1,436 r13

Page 24
1. 30
2. 44
3. 29
4. 24
5. 52
6. 61
7. 42
8. 56
9. 55
10. 65
11. 58
12. 37

Page 25
1.
```
      19 r2
  5) 97
 100 ÷ 5 = 20
```
2.
```
      902 r3
  6) 5,415
 5,400 ÷ 6 = 900
```

Page 25 (continued)
3.
```
      37 r1
 11) 408
 400 ÷ 10 = 40
```
4.
```
      31 r2
 67) 2,079
 2,100 ÷ 70 = 30
```
5.
```
      679 r13
 82) 55,691
 56,000 ÷ 80 = 700
```
6.
```
      3,141 r12
 29) 91,101
 90,000 ÷ 30 = 3,000
```

Page 26
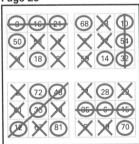

Page 27

Page 28

Page 29
1. 14, 98, 686
2. 55, 605, 6,655
3. 36 r7
4. 458 r6
5. 1,157 r3
6. 3,063 r6

Answers

Page 30
1.
$$72\overline{)3{,}530}\ \ 49\ \text{r}2$$
3,500 ÷ 70 = 50

2.
$$23\overline{)47{,}897}\ \ 2{,}082\ \text{r}11$$
48,000 ÷ 24 = 2,000

3. 29, 7, 31, 13, 5, 71, 19
4. 18, 54, 82, 35, 66, 20, 72

Page 31
1. 7, 3, 6, 1, 2, 4, 8
2. 9, 4, 8, 2, 1, 5, 6
3. 0, 0, 2, 4, 8, 1, 7
4. 8, 2, 1, 0, 5, 3, 9
5. 4, 1, 9, 4, 6, 8, 2
6. 1, 5, 7, 6, 0, 4, 1

Page 32
1. hundreds
2. tenths
3. thousandths
4. ones
5. thousands
6. hundredths
7. tens
8. tenths
9. hundreds
10. thousandths

Page 33
1. 4.914, 4.952, 5.279, 5.836
2. 7.156, 7.159, 7.671, 8.442
3. 0.482, 0.533, 0.617, 0.694
4. 1.208, 1.228, 1.232, 1.265
5. 4.003, 4.006, 4.014, 4.053
6. 0.239, 0.322, 0.329, 0.932

Page 34
1. > 2. = 3. > 4. <
5. < 6. > 7. < 8. <
9. > 10. < 11. = 12. >
13. < 14. > 15. > 16. <
17. < 18. > 19. < 20. =

Page 35
1. 1 2. 9 3. 6 4. 4
5. 5 6. 4 7. 5 8. 10
9. 3 10. 9 11. 0 12. 8
13. 6 14. 3 15. 1 16. 7

Page 36
1. 11.79, 12.00
2. 3.12, 3.00
3. 9.85, 10.00
4. 20.28, 20.00
5. 5.41, 5.00
6. 10.50, 11.00

Page 37
1. 2.2   2. 5.7
3. 8.2   4. 1.8
5. 3.3   6. 7.7
7. 4.1   8. 0
9. 9.55   10. 4.48
11. 1.92 12. 4.53
13. 2.38 14. 5.17
15. 3.09 16. 6.90

Page 38

	Nearest One	Nearest Tenth	Nearest Hundredth
25.158	25	25.2	25.16
1.372	1	1.4	1.37
83.614	84	83.6	83.61
390.293	390	390.3	390.29
7.872	8	7.9	7.87
14.426	14	14.4	14.43
5.555	6	5.6	5.56
0.307	0	0.3	0.31

Page 39
1. 9.76   2. 29.55
3. 87.48   4. 58.25
5. 189.87   6. 975.63
7. 5.31   8. 62.23
9. 45.02   10. 24.44
11. 511.90 12. 237.57

Page 40
1. 9.5   2. 11.62
3. 40.84   4. 87.02
5. 108.55   6. 105.387
7. 151.557   8. 675.31
9. 1,366.84 10. 738.362
11. 2,930.382 12. 10,044.42

Page 41
1. 3.4   2. 2.78
3. 58.96   4. 17.931
5. 48.51   6. 535.47
7. 754.37   8. 27.649
9. 471.56   10. 583.248
11. 1,979.78 12. 7,768.15

Page 42
1.
$$\begin{array}{r} 3.42 \\ +5.6 \\ \hline 9.02 \end{array} \qquad \begin{array}{r} 3 \\ +6 \\ \hline 9 \end{array}$$

2.
$$\begin{array}{r} 1.84 \\ +4.95 \\ \hline 6.79 \end{array} \qquad \begin{array}{r} 2 \\ +5 \\ \hline 7 \end{array}$$

3.
$$\begin{array}{r} 4.068 \\ +6.75 \\ \hline 10.818 \end{array} \qquad \begin{array}{r} 4 \\ +7 \\ \hline 11 \end{array}$$

4.
$$\begin{array}{r} 6.17 \\ -2.9 \\ \hline 3.27 \end{array} \qquad \begin{array}{r} 6 \\ -3 \\ \hline 3 \end{array}$$

5.
$$\begin{array}{r} 9.81 \\ -5.66 \\ \hline 4.15 \end{array} \qquad \begin{array}{r} 10 \\ -6 \\ \hline 4 \end{array}$$

6.
$$\begin{array}{r} 12.691 \\ -4.32 \\ \hline 8.371 \end{array} \qquad \begin{array}{r} 13 \\ -4 \\ \hline 9 \end{array}$$

Page 43
1. 13.3   2. 36.5
3. 25.89   4. 124.2
5. 21.12   6. 56.28
7. 19.38   8. 9.75
9. 18.767   10. 0.352
11. 44.064 12. 59.93

Page 44
1. 0.7   2. 0.4
3. 1.67   4. 3.27
5. 2.91   6. 4.32
7. 3.117   8. 0.574
9. 5.86   10. 3.45
11. 0.263   12. 0.174

Page 45
Suggested estimates:
1. 4 × 7 = 28
2. 4 × 4 = 16
3. 5 × 8 = 40
4. 3 × 40 = 120
5. 4 × 11 = 44
6. 9 × 9 = 81
7. 6 ÷ 6 = 1
8. 4.8 ÷ 8 = 0.6
9. 9.3 ÷ 3 = 3.1
10. 1.2 ÷ 6 = 0.2
11. 4.5 ÷ 5 = 0.9
12. 110 ÷ 11 = 10

Page 46
1. 45.1   2. 19.83
3. 724.2   4. 60.3
5. 8,599   6. 4,217
7. 0.36   8. 7.738
9. 9.366   10. 541.03
11. 38.249   12. 0.572

Page 47
1. >   2. <   3. =
4. <   5. >   6. >
7. <   8. <   9. =
10. <   11. 5   12. 9
13. 35   14. 1   15. 6.6
16. 25.9 17. 0.8   18. 7.6
19. 5.98 20. 0.16 21. 5.91
22. 0.01

Page 48
Suggested estimates:
1. 11   2. 7   3. 12
4. 0.9   5. 9   6. 12
7. 70   8. 5
9. 37.93   10. 623.09
11. 17.574 12. 2.41
13. 1,025.20 14. 175.166
15. 1,443.015 16. 0.521
17. 782   18. 345
19. 449.82 20. 9.2

Page 49
1. $\frac{1}{6}$ 2. $\frac{5}{8}$ 3. $\frac{3}{4}$
4. $\frac{2}{5}$ 5. $\frac{7}{8}$ 6. $\frac{3}{7}$
7. $\frac{3}{4}$, $\frac{3}{7}$ 8. $\frac{5}{8}$, $\frac{7}{8}$

Page 50
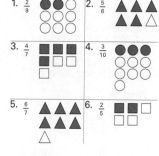
1. $\frac{2}{9}$ 2. $\frac{5}{6}$
3. $\frac{4}{7}$ 4. $\frac{3}{10}$
5. $\frac{6}{7}$ 6. $\frac{2}{5}$
7. $\frac{2}{9}$, $\frac{2}{5}$ 8. $\frac{4}{7}$, $\frac{6}{7}$

Page 51
1. $\frac{3}{9}$ 2. $\frac{3}{4}$
3. $\frac{2}{10}$ 4. $\frac{1}{3}$

Page 52
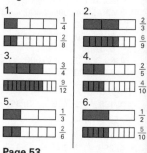
1. $\frac{1}{4}$, $\frac{2}{8}$
2. $\frac{2}{3}$, $\frac{6}{9}$
3. $\frac{3}{4}$, $\frac{9}{12}$
4. $\frac{2}{5}$, $\frac{4}{10}$
5. $\frac{1}{3}$, $\frac{2}{6}$
6. $\frac{1}{2}$, $\frac{5}{10}$

Page 53
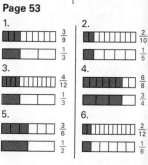
1. $\frac{3}{9}$, $\frac{1}{3}$
2. $\frac{2}{10}$, $\frac{1}{5}$
3. $\frac{4}{12}$, $\frac{1}{3}$
4. $\frac{6}{8}$, $\frac{3}{4}$
5. $\frac{3}{6}$, $\frac{1}{2}$
6. $\frac{2}{12}$, $\frac{1}{6}$

Page 54
1. $\frac{2}{3}$ 2. $\frac{1}{2}$ 3. $\frac{1}{3}$
4. $\frac{1}{4}$ 5. $\frac{2}{5}$ 6. $\frac{3}{4}$
7. $\frac{5}{6}$ 8. $\frac{4}{9}$ 9. $\frac{7}{8}$
10. $\frac{3}{5}$ 11. $\frac{4}{7}$ 12. $\frac{9}{10}$

Page 55
1. $1\frac{6}{7}$ 2. $2\frac{1}{4}$ 3. $1\frac{4}{9}$
4. $2\frac{2}{5}$ 5. $3\frac{1}{2}$ 6. $3\frac{5}{8}$

Page 56
1. $2\frac{3}{4}$ 2. $4\frac{4}{5}$ 3. $6\frac{1}{3}$
4. $4\frac{1}{2}$ 5. $7\frac{3}{7}$ 6. $1\frac{1}{10}$
7. $10\frac{5}{6}$ 8. $5\frac{3}{8}$ 9. $7\frac{2}{3}$
10. $3\frac{4}{9}$ 11. $11\frac{2}{5}$ 12. $3\frac{7}{12}$

Page 57
1. $\frac{17}{2}$ 2. $\frac{13}{6}$ 3. $\frac{31}{4}$
4. $\frac{11}{3}$ 5. $\frac{92}{9}$ 6. $\frac{25}{6}$
7. $\frac{43}{8}$ 8. $\frac{32}{5}$ 9. $\frac{34}{11}$
10. $\frac{37}{4}$ 11. $\frac{44}{10}$ 12. $\frac{79}{9}$

Answers

Page 58
1. $1\frac{2}{5}$ 2. $\frac{27}{8}$ 3. $\frac{10}{3}$
4. $2\frac{3}{10}$ 5. $7\frac{3}{7}$ 6. $6\frac{3}{4}$

Page 59
1. $\frac{1}{10}$, 0.1 2. $\frac{4}{10}$, 0.4
3. $\frac{9}{10}$, 0.9 4. $\frac{5}{10}$, 0.5
5. $\frac{7}{10}$, 0.7 6. $\frac{6}{10}$, 0.6

Page 60
1. $\frac{55}{100}$, 0.55 2. $\frac{28}{100}$, 0.28
3. $\frac{96}{100}$, 0.96 4. $\frac{8}{100}$, 0.08

Page 61
1. $\frac{13}{100}$, 13% 2. $\frac{88}{100}$, 88%
3. $\frac{39}{100}$, 39% 4. $\frac{61}{100}$, 61%

Page 62
1. 60% 2. 32% 3. 20%
4. 50% 5. 48% 6. 15%
7. $\frac{7}{50}$ 8. $\frac{2}{5}$ 9. $\frac{9}{25}$
10. $\frac{1}{10}$ 11. $\frac{7}{20}$ 12. $\frac{23}{100}$

Page 63
1. 20% 2. 45% 3. 99%
4. 13% 5. 51% 6. 88%
7. 27% 8. 6% 9. 39%
10. 21% 11. 72% 12. 63%
13. 0.75 14. 0.46 15. 0.32
16. 0.93 17. 0.08 18. 0.15
19. 0.84 20. 0.01 21. 0.51
22. 0.27 23. 0.68 24. 0.82

Page 64
1. 36 2. 21 3. 13
4. 7.5 5. 5.46 6. 33.6
7. 3.52 8. 35.15 9. 4.35

Page 65
1. 0.45 2. 0.7
3.

4. 100% 5. $\frac{3}{8}$

Page 66
1. = 2. > 3. < 4. >
5. < 6. > 7. < 8. =
9. > 10. = 11. > 12. <
13. < 14. < 15. = 16. <

Page 67
1. $\frac{6}{10}$, $\frac{15}{25}$, $\frac{30}{50}$
2. $\frac{1}{2}$ 3. $\frac{7}{9}$ 4. $\frac{3}{10}$
5. $\frac{5}{6}$ 6. $2\frac{1}{5}$ 7. $9\frac{2}{7}$
8. $4\frac{3}{10}$ 9. $3\frac{2}{9}$ 10. $\frac{12}{7}$
11. $\frac{23}{6}$ 12. $\frac{33}{4}$ 13. $\frac{46}{11}$

Page 68

Percent	Decimal	Fraction
70%	0.7	$\frac{7}{10}$
20%	0.2	$\frac{1}{5}$
80%	0.8	$\frac{4}{5}$
35%	0.35	$\frac{7}{20}$
66%	0.66	$\frac{33}{50}$
4%	0.04	$\frac{1}{25}$

1. 15.6 2. 11.61 3. 93.06

Page 69
1. $\frac{4}{5}$ 2. $\frac{6}{7}$ 3. $\frac{10}{11}$
4. $\frac{8}{8}$ 5. $\frac{9}{14}$

Page 70
1. $2\frac{2}{3}$ 2. $\frac{1}{2}$ 3. $1\frac{5}{9}$
4. $\frac{5}{6}$ 5. $4\frac{3}{8}$ 6. $\frac{2}{3}$
7. 7 8. $\frac{7}{9}$ 9. $5\frac{1}{4}$
10. $1\frac{3}{5}$

Page 71
1. $1\frac{1}{6}$ 2. $\frac{1}{3}$ 3. $3\frac{1}{8}$
4. $1\frac{3}{20}$ 5. $2\frac{2}{9}$ 6. $1\frac{7}{16}$
7. 2 8. $1\frac{11}{36}$ 9. $2\frac{1}{8}$

Page 72
1. $7\frac{4}{7}$ 2. $6\frac{5}{8}$ 3. $8\frac{14}{15}$
4. $9\frac{8}{9}$ 5. $3\frac{7}{10}$ 6. $6\frac{5}{6}$
7. $8\frac{1}{2}$ 8. $12\frac{3}{8}$ 9. $16\frac{1}{14}$

Page 73
1. $\frac{1}{5}$ 2. $\frac{3}{10}$ 3. $\frac{2}{6}$
4. $\frac{5}{12}$ 5. $\frac{5}{8}$ 6. $\frac{2}{9}$

Page 74
1. $\frac{1}{2}$ 2. $\frac{3}{4}$ 3. $\frac{1}{3}$
4. $\frac{1}{9}$ 5. $\frac{11}{12}$ 6. 1
7. $1\frac{2}{13}$ 8. $3\frac{1}{9}$ 9. $1\frac{1}{5}$
10. $\frac{3}{4}$

Page 75
1. $\frac{1}{10}$ 2. $\frac{7}{12}$ 3. $\frac{11}{40}$
4. $\frac{1}{6}$ 5. $\frac{1}{9}$ 6. $\frac{11}{24}$
7. $1\frac{1}{2}$ 8. $1\frac{2}{15}$ 9. $3\frac{9}{20}$

Page 76
1. $2\frac{1}{7}$ 2. $7\frac{2}{3}$ 3. $3\frac{1}{2}$
4. $1\frac{1}{10}$ 5. $9\frac{1}{9}$ 6. $4\frac{3}{14}$
7. $2\frac{5}{8}$ 8. $\frac{2}{3}$ 9. $5\frac{17}{18}$

Page 77
1. 1 2. 5 3. 3
4. $\frac{1}{5}$ 5. $\frac{1}{8}$ 6. $\frac{2}{9}$

Page 78
1. $\frac{1}{15}$ 2. $\frac{1}{10}$ 3. $\frac{2}{7}$
4. $\frac{10}{27}$ 5. $\frac{1}{4}$ 6. $\frac{1}{20}$
7. $\frac{9}{28}$ 8. $\frac{1}{14}$ 9. $\frac{3}{16}$

Page 79
1. $\frac{3}{10}$ 2. $\frac{5}{28}$ 3. $\frac{5}{11}$
4. $\frac{9}{32}$ 5. $\frac{7}{8}$ 6. $\frac{11}{36}$
7. $\frac{1}{6}$ 8. $\frac{3}{4}$ 9. $\frac{2}{9}$

Page 80
1. $3\frac{1}{9}$ 2. $15\frac{3}{4}$ 3. 6
4. $7\frac{1}{3}$ 5. 8 6. $16\frac{1}{2}$
7. $21\frac{2}{3}$ 8. $5\frac{1}{4}$ 9. 68

Page 81
1. $\frac{6}{5}$ 2. $\frac{2}{7}$ 3. $\frac{3}{1}$
4. $\frac{10}{9}$ 5. $\frac{5}{12}$ 6. $\frac{11}{1}$
7. $\frac{5}{8}$ 8. $\frac{1}{8}$ 9. $\frac{13}{4}$
10. $\frac{23}{32}$ 11. $\frac{67}{55}$ 12. $\frac{100}{99}$

Page 82
1. 1 2. 1 3. 1
4. $\frac{3}{4}$ 5. $\frac{9}{8}$ 6. $\frac{1}{3}$
7. $\frac{6}{17}$ 8. $\frac{103}{78}$ 9. $\frac{6}{35}$

Page 83
1. 12 2. 10 3. 5
4. 3 5. 4 6. 2

Page 84
1. $1\frac{7}{8}$ 2. $\frac{1}{4}$ 3. $\frac{7}{12}$
4. $\frac{1}{8}$ 5. $6\frac{2}{3}$ 6. $\frac{1}{2}$
7. $\frac{3}{4}$ 8. $5\frac{5}{6}$ 9. $1\frac{1}{3}$

Page 85
1. $1\frac{1}{2}$ 2. $\frac{2}{9}$ 3. $1\frac{2}{21}$
4. $\frac{4}{9}$ 5. $1\frac{1}{17}$ 6. $\frac{7}{12}$
7. $2\frac{1}{2}$ 8. $2\frac{1}{9}$ 9. $\frac{5}{27}$

Page 86
1. 74 2. 96 3. 120
4. 360 5. 104 6. 180
7. 369 8. 90

Page 87
1. 1 2. $1\frac{2}{9}$ 3. $\frac{2}{3}$
4. $1\frac{5}{21}$ 5. $7\frac{8}{9}$ 6. $12\frac{5}{16}$
7. $\frac{3}{13}$ 8. $\frac{1}{2}$ 9. $\frac{1}{16}$
10. $\frac{7}{15}$ 11. $4\frac{1}{9}$ 12. $6\frac{17}{35}$

Answers

Page 88
1. $\frac{1}{12}$ 2. $\frac{1}{54}$ 3. $\frac{3}{8}$

4. 1   5. 1   6. $17\frac{1}{5}$

7. $\frac{4}{7}$ 8. $1\frac{1}{5}$ 9. $1\frac{5}{7}$

10. $\frac{2}{3}$ 11. 18   12. $\frac{1}{30}$

Page 89
1. $4\frac{1}{2}$ 2. $6\frac{3}{4}$ 3. $2\frac{2}{3}$

4. $1\frac{7}{9}$ 5. 8   6. $5\frac{1}{3}$

Page 90
1. 2.5   2. 1.5   3. 0.9
4. 18   5. 30   6. 50
7. 54   8. 90   9. 150

Page 91
1. 18   2. 60
3. 65.6   4. 40

Page 92
1. 36   2. 274
3. 58   4. 22.2

Page 93
1. right   2. obtuse   3. acute
4. obtuse   5. acute   6. right
7. acute   8. obtuse   9. obtuse

Page 94
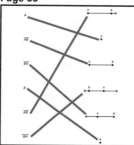

Page 95

Right Angles	Acute Angles	Obtuse Angles
4	0	0
1	2	0
0	2	2
0	0	8
0	2	2
1	1	3

Page 96
1. 15   2. 120   3. 87
4. 163   5. 38   6. 142

Page 97
1. ray
2. line segment
3. point
4. line
5. ray

Page 98
1. $\overleftrightarrow{AB}$ 2. $\overrightarrow{QR}$ 3. F
4. $\overrightarrow{MN}$ 5. $\overline{CD}$ 6. $\overleftrightarrow{KL}$
7. X 8. $\overrightarrow{GH}$ 9. $\overrightarrow{YZ}$

Page 99
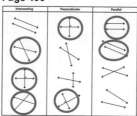

Page 100
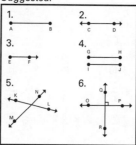

Page 101
1. parallel
2. intersecting
3. intersecting, perpendicular
4. parallel
5. intersecting, perpendicular
6. intersecting, perpendicular
7. intersecting

Page 102
Suggested:
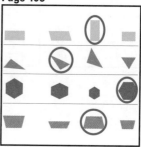

Page 103
1. hexagon
2. quadrilateral
3. decagon
4. heptagon
5. quadrilateral
6. nonagon
7. pentagon
8. octagon

Page 104
1. rhombus, parallelogram
2. square, rectangle
3. trapezoid
4. parallelogram
5. rectangle
6. rhombus, parallelogram
7. parallelogram
8. trapezoid

Page 105

Shape Name	Sides	Vertices	Pairs of Parallel Lines
parallelogram	4	4	2
hexagon	6	6	3
nonagon	9	9	0
trapezoid	4	4	1
pentagon	5	5	0

Page 106

Page 107
1. 70   2. 25   3. 644
4. 480   5. 30   6. 23.04

Page 108
1. 9   2. 48   3. 40
4. 105   5. $6\frac{1}{2}$ 6. 75.33

Page 109
1. 15   2. 120   3. 81
4. 391   5. $11\frac{1}{9}$ 6. 45.08

Page 110
1. 23   2. 70
3. 96   4. 327

Page 111
1. sphere
2. square pyramid
3. cone
4. cube
5. rectangular prism
6. cylinder

Page 112

Shape Name	Vertices	Edges	Faces
rectangular prism	8	12	6
square pyramid	5	8	5
cube	8	12	6

Page 113
1. 4   2. 15   3. 24
4. 27   5. 24   6. 20

Page 114
1. 216   2. 160   3. 1,859
4. 4,500   5. 90   6. 167.44

Page 115
1. 385   2. 1,690
3. 1,734   4. $370\frac{1}{2}$
5. 875   6. 945
7. flower planter
8. cereal box

Page 116
1. 1,457   2. 750
3. 1,476   4. 1,826

Page 117
1. square pyramid
2. obtuse angle
3. point
4. pentagon
5. line segment
6. heptagon
7. cylinder
8. parallel lines
9. acute angle
10. ray
11. perpendicular lines
12. sphere

Page 118
1. 82°   2. 155°
3. 13°   4. 26, 40
5. 28, 36   6. 36, 54
7. 135   8. 355.32
9. $48\frac{3}{4}$

Photo by Pete Perry

ABOUT THE AUTHOR

Lee Weinstein is a former Nike public relations leader who is now an entrepreneur. He has worked for a United States congressman and an Oregon governor and served on numerous nonprofit boards of directors.

Lee, who is president of PR Boutiques International—an association of 40 PR boutique agencies worldwide—is an experienced facilitator and frequent public speaker. He and his wife, Melinda, teach Intentional Life Planning workshops, based on the process they developed in 2000. Lee's article "The Restless Soul in the Bathroom Mirror," about his career relaunch, which occurred because of this Intentional Life Planning approach, was published in *The New York Times*. He regularly counsels job seekers on finding their path.

Lee and Melinda own Weinstein PR, a boutique public relations agency based in Portland, Ore., and the Columbia River Gorge National Scenic Area. They have two daughters, Emma and Sophie, and live in The Dalles.

Illustration Credits

Page 15. "Remember: You Will Die" based on "The Accurate" watch from Mr Jones Watches.

Page 16. "What Matters the Most" based on the original idea, text and Dharma doodle by Eric Klein, wisdomheart.com. Used by permission.

Page 101. "My Plan; What Actually Happened" based on the original idea and doodle by Julia Gamolina. Used by permission.

Join Our Community

writeopenact.com

Facebook.com/writeopenact

Twitter.com/writeopenact

Instagram.com/writeopenact

Use 'Write, Open, Act' in Your Book Group

Email info@writeopenact.com for a guide

"I'VE LEARNED THAT PEOPLE WILL FORGET WHAT YOU SAID, PEOPLE WILL FORGET WHAT YOU DID, BUT PEOPLE WILL NEVER FORGET HOW YOU MADE THEM FEEL."

—Maya Angelou